![Barefoot Collective logo]

BAREFOOT COLLECTIVE

Praise for The Barefoot Guides

"The Barefoot Guides use simple methodologies that allow people to bring the best of their experiences to share through the book. They show that all we need is to be awake to learn, to create, to innovate and by the end of day we can create a transformational approach. All of us can do it, even those who do not know they can, truly they can do it too… all of us can change lives!"

> Mário Albino Machimbene, KEPA, Maputo City, Mozambique

"This exceptional series is hugely accessible yet deeply rooted in solid theory and extensive practice across a wide range of contexts and fields. Expect from it something truly unique in its combination of insight, reflection, experience and highly usable mixed text/visual presentation. It is not "dumbed down." I have seen it bite as deeply at high academic and professional level as well as at grassroots community leadership level -- an astonishing achievement worth honouring."

> James R. Cochrane, Emeritus Professor, Religious Studies, University of Cape Town, and Adjunct Professor, Dept of Social Sciences and Health Policy, Wake Forest School of Medicine, USA

"The Barefoot Guides are chock-full of practical wisdom. It has given more legitimacy to a way of working that has always felt 'true' and 'right' to me intuitively and that I have seen the effectiveness of in action."

> Tana Paddock, Organization Unbound, Cape Town, South Africa

"The Barefoot Guide Connection has a unique and truly transformational approach to collaboration, learning and facilitating social, transformational change across borders."

> Tobias Troll, Director, EDGE Europe at EDGE Funders Alliance, Brussels, Belgium

"The Barefoot Guides are an important reference for our international students in development studies. Crossing the border between academia and practitioners, they repeatedly prove to be a rich source of inspiration for those working with local communities and grassroots organizations"

> Dr Kees Biekart, International Institute of Social Studies (ISS) of Erasmus University, the Hague, Netherlands

"The Barefoot Guides are a wonderful contribution to open access knowledge, grounded on a great depth of experience and horizontal learning from across the world."

> Samantha Button, Maliasili Initiatives, Tanzania

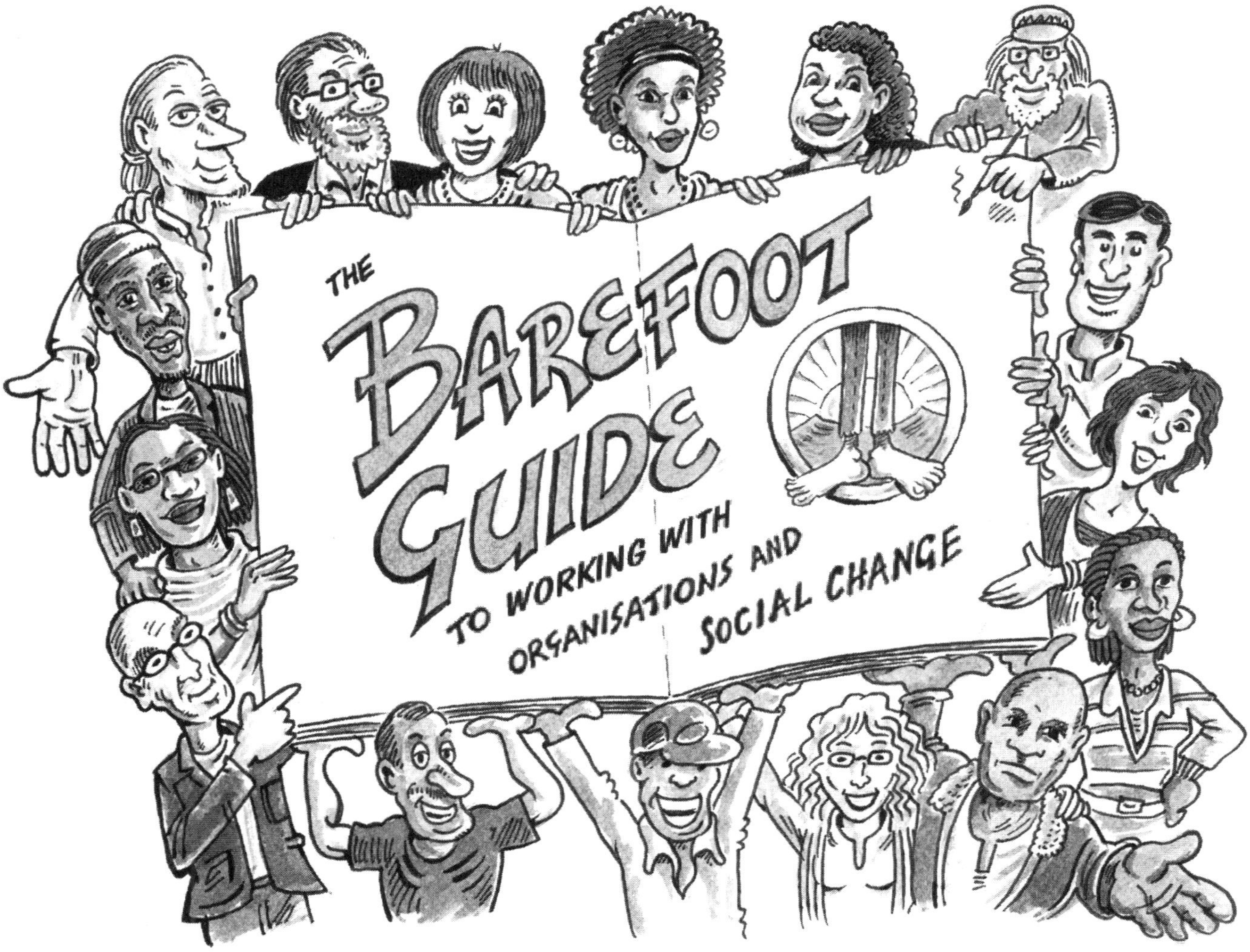

The Barefoot Guide Writers' Collective

Illustrated by

N. D. MAZIN

Practical Action Publishing Ltd
The Schumacher Centre
Bourton on Dunsmore, Rugby,
Warwickshire CV23 9QZ, UK
www.practicalactionpublishing.org

Copyright © The Barefoot Guide Writers' Collective, 2009

First published by Barefoot Guide Connection in 2009
This edition published by Practical Action Publishing in 2016

ISBN   978-1-85339-714-1 Paperback

The Barefoot Guide to Working with Organisations and Social Change by the Barefoot Writers' Collective is licensed under a Creative Commons Attribution-Non-Commercial-Share Alike 3.0 Unported License. This allows the reader to copy and redistribute the material, and to adapt the work, but appropriate credit must be given, the material must not be used for commercial purposes, and if the material is transformed or built upon the modified material may only be distributed under the same or similar license to this one. For further information see https://creativecommons.org/licenses/by-nc-sa/3.0/

A catalogue record for this book is available from the British Library.

The contributors have asserted their rights under the Copyright Designs and Patents Act 1988 to be identified as authors of the work.

The Barefoot Guide Writers' Collective, (2016) *The Barefoot Guide to Working with Organisations and Social Change*, Rugby, UK: Practical Action Publishing.

Since 1974, Practical Action Publishing has published and disseminated books and information in support of international development work throughout the world. Practical Action Publishing is a trading name of Practical Action Publishing Ltd (Company Reg. No. 1159018), the wholly owned publishing company of Practical Action. Practical Action Publishing trades only in support of its parent charity objectives and any profits are covenanted back to Practical Action (Charity Reg. No. 247257, Group VAT Registration No. 880 9924 76).

The views and opinions in this publication are those of the author and do not represent those of Practical Action Publishing Ltd or its parent charity Practical Action. Reasonable efforts have been made to publish reliable data and information, but the authors and publisher cannot assume responsibility for the validity of all materials or for the consequences of their use.

Printed in the United Kingdom

Contents

1 Introduction — Welcome
What is the Barefoot Guide?
The People Of The Barefoot Collective
Honouring The Sources Of This Guide
Copyright And Licensing

7 Chapter One — Shaping Our World
New Ways Of Looking At Organisations And Social Change

Why Organisations Matter
Seeing What Is There, Supporting What Is Possible
Seeing The Future In Sovereign Local Organisations
Key Aspects Of Sovereign Organisations
Seeing Organisations: Machines or Living Systems?
Key Principles and Ideas Guiding this Book
Seeing the Ways Organisations Change
Seeing the Future Organisation of Society

23 Chapter Two — Inside Out
Towards understanding ourselves, other people and how we change

Asking Good Questions
Good Facilitation And Facilitative Leadership
The Threefold Human Being
Phases Of Individual Development
The Four Temperaments
Leadership Polarities

47 Chapter Three — People to People
Creating and Working with Relationships in Organisation

Why Are Relationships So Important?
Seeing Through Relationships
Power, Relationships, Change
Types Of Power
Five Bases Of Power

Why Is It Important For Us To Talk About Power?
What Is Needed?
What can Get In The Way?
Some Practical Tips

65 Chapter Four — Through the Looking Glass
Observing and Understanding Organisations

Facilitating Organisational Understanding — Some Principles And Guidelines
Does Organisational Assessment Help Anyone?
The Phases Of Organisation Development
Using Phases Of Development In Practice
Organisational Elements And Cycles
Getting Practical — Techniques For Observing And Understanding Organisations

101 Chapter Five — Stepping into the Unknown
Facilitating Change in Organisation

Common Issues In Facilitating Change
Facilitating Emergent Change
Using The Action Learning Cycle As A Tool
Facilitating Transformative Change
The Seven Tasks Of Working Through The U-Process
Facilitating Projectable Change
3 Key Challenges Of The Project Cycle
Drawing The Threads Together

125 Chapter Six — Finding a home for change
Supporting, Grounding and Sustaining Change

Why Is Organisational Change So Difficult To Accomplish?
Managing The Transitions Of Transformative Change
Practical Suggestions For Leaders In Implementing Change

135 Chapter Seven — Staying alive to change
Learning and Innovating in Organisations

What Does It Mean To Be A Learning Organisation?
Designing Our Own Approach To Learning In Organisation
Practical Guidelines for Designing Learning
Watch Out For…
Why Do Organisations Resist Learning?
Key Elements Of Organisational Learning
Stories, Learning And Social Change…
Planning, Monitoring and Evaluation (PME)
Mapping PME in the Development Sector
Outcome Mapping
Horizontal Learning — And New Forms Of Organisation…

INTRODUCTION
Welcome!

...to The Barefoot Guide to Working With Organisations and Social Change

Please take off your shoes...

What is this Barefoot Guide?

This is a practical, do-it-yourself guide for leaders and facilitators wanting to help organisations to function and to develop in more healthy, human and effective ways as they strive to make their contributions to a more humane society. It has been developed by the Barefoot Collective.

The guide, with its supporting website, includes tried and tested concepts, approaches, stories and activities. Its purpose is to help stimulate and enrich the practice of anyone supporting organisations and social movements in their challenges of working, learning, growing and changing to meet the needs of our complex world. Although it is aimed at leaders and facilitators of civil society organisations, we hope it will be useful to anyone interested in fostering healthy human organisation in any sphere of life.

The Barefoot Guide is offered free to the world and can be downloaded on this website: www.barefootguide.org. The website also contains a growing library of additional downloadable exercises, readings, case studies and diagrams to accompany the Barefoot Guide.

In this book we offer a perspective on why organisations exist, the real roles they play, and on the importance of supporting the sovereignty of local organisations and social movements for meaningful social change. You will find here a range of approaches to understanding ourselves and our roles as leaders and facilitators, as we try to understand and facilitate change in organisations. In addition, the significance of relationships and power dynamics in organisations and organisational change processes are explored. We provide some tools for reading organisations, including how organisations tend to move through various phases of development, how we might facilitate change and the challenges we all face in implementing or sustaining change. Finally, the guide gives support to processes of building learning organisations, how we can continually learn both from our own experiences and the experiences of others.

WHO IS THE BAREFOOT COLLECTIVE?

This guide is offered to you by a global team of collaborating practitioners and activists from the Community Development Resource Association (South Africa), Voluntary Service Overseas (Nepal, Cameroon, Canada), ActionAid (Ghana, India), the Treatment Action Campaign (South Africa) and the Church Land Programme (South Africa) and some independent practitioners. Valuable contributions were also received from The Democracy Development Programme (South Africa) and Oxfam UK.

WE NEED YOUR FEEDBACK

We see this guide as a work in progress to be annually updated, based on feedback and contributions from users.

We are releasing this Pilot Edition with an invitation to anyone who uses it to send us your comments, based on your own experience. We are keen that this guide is tested in many different contexts. This will help us to expand our understanding of the real work that leaders and facilitators are facing and thus enable us to improve the guide.

Our thinking at this stage is to produce revised editions annually – perhaps until this guide outgrows us and becomes something else entirely! If it is found to be useful enough we plan to have it translated into various languages and also produce a colour hard-cover version for sale.

Our website (www.barefootguide.org) has an online feedback form. You can also email Tracey Martin, who is leading the feedback process, with your feedback, comments and suggestions – feedback@barefootguide.org

FEEDBACK QUESTIONS:

1. Has the Guide inspired any changes in how you do something or approach your work? It would be helpful if you could tell us a brief story of how you have used the Guide and what responses it has had.
2. Which chapters have been particularly helpful? Why?
3. Is there anything else that you would like to see in the Guide?
4. Is there any part of the Guide that you have found difficult to understand?
5. Is there anything in the Guide that you disagree with? Please tell us why and suggest or feel free to contribute alternatives.

Send your feedback to feedback@barefootguide.org

CONTRIBUTE YOUR TOOLS AND RESOURCES

We also welcome additional materials for future editions and for the website. These could be - activities, readings, case stories or even poems or images that you'd like to contribute that you have found useful and might be useful to others. We can't promise that we will always include them, but each contribution will be seriously considered and acknowledged, if used.

Email your contributions to contact@barefootguide.org

The People of the Barefoot Collective

The People of the Barefoot Collective

Initiating writers: Doug Reeler, Rubert Van Blerk, James Taylor, Desiree Paulsen, Sue Soal (CDRA, South Africa)
Editor and Cartoonist: Andy Mason
Co-writers: Catherine Collingwood (Independent practitioner, South Africa) Christine Mylks (VSO International), Maureen Mbuyongha Anfumbom (VSO Cameroon), Phakama Pyoos, Karabo Monatisi, Khayalethu Mofu (TAC, South Africa), Manas Ranjan (ActionAid India), Nomusa Sokhela (Church Land Programme, South Africa), Saani Yakuba (ActionAid Ghana), Simon Brown, Tracey Martin (VSO Nepal)

Website: Laura Garcia-Puig (VSO Nepal), Urs Hauptle
Layout Artist: Paula Wood (Paula Wood Design, South Africa)
Administration and finance: Linda Njambatwa and Vernon Weitz, (CDRA)
Contributions: Rama Naidoo (The Democracy Development Programme, South Africa) and Azer Hasanov (Oxfam UK)

CONTACT US
Please contact us via email – contact@barefootguide.org

Honouring the sources of this Guide

The ideas in this Guide come from many different sources. We have drawn from the published ideas of others, from those who have worked with us, from our own experiences and what we have learned from a whole host of practitioners over the years, in many countries and settings. We have taken ideas, worked with them and adapted them, based on real experience in the field. It is almost impossible to trace or fully acknowledge the rich history of what is reflected in these pages.

But we would like to make special mention of the Anthroposophical impulse and in particular Rudolf Steiner and Bernard Lievegoed, whose ideas of human development have filtered into a whole school of thought about the development of people, organisations and society.

Members of the NPI Institute of Organisation Development (www.npi-academie.nl), which was founded by Bernard Lievegoed in 1954, also deserve special mention. They have worked with this impulse and added and developed their own ideas and concepts several, of which are to be found in this guide. Among many they are Mario van Boeschoten, Fritz Glasl, Dik Crum, and Leo de la Houssaye. David Scott worked with CDRA for many years and introduced us to several of these exercises and concepts.

The particular concepts we have used, associated with these practitioners and where they are in this Guide are:

- The Three Fold Human being - Rudolph Steiner
- Phases of Human Development and Biography Work - Bernard Lievegoed and Mario van Boeschoten
- Phases of Organisation Development - Bernard Lievegoed and Fritz Glasl
- Four Temperaments - Rudolph Steiner and Dik Crum
- Leadership Polarities - Leo de la Houssaye
- U-process - Fritz Glasl

It is quite possible that we have missed some acknowledgement here and look forward to being corrected, for future revisions of the Guide.

COPYRIGHT and LICENSING

This book is available as a FREE download from the barefootguide website. Please keep it that way. No portion of the text, graphics or cartoons in this book may be used for commercial purposes.

The intention of the Barefoot Collective is that users of this book should feel free to copy and distribute it, in any form, printed or electronic, strictly for non-profit purposes. You can distribute it either as a whole book or in parts - some pages are ideal to be photocopied as hand-outs.

If you wish to use any parts of this book in the creation of your own materials, please ensure that the Barefoot Guide, the Barefoot Collective, and the illustrator, N.D. Mazin, are properly acknowledged. Please include the website address, www.barefootguide.org.

Please feel free to include a link from your website to the barefootguide.org website. Please do not host the book's download files on your website as we will be bringing out corrected and updated versions from time to time.

Please email us at contact@barefootguide.org to discuss the above.

Legalese

The Barefoot Guide to Working with Organisations and Social Change by the Barefoot Collective is licensed under a Creative Commons Attribution-Non-Commercial-Share Alike 3.0 Unported License. Permissions beyond the scope of this license may be available at www.barefootguide.org.

YOU ARE FREE:

- to Share - to copy, distribute and transmit the work
- to Remix - to adapt the work

Under the following conditions:

- Attribution. You must attribute the work in the manner specified by the author or licensor (but not in any way that suggests that they endorse you or your use of the work).
- Noncommercial. You may not use this work for commercial purposes.
- Share Alike. If you alter, transform, or build upon this work, you may distribute the resulting work only under the same or similar license to this one.

For any reuse or distribution, you must make clear to others the license terms of this work. The best way to do this is with a link to this web page.

The above conditions may only be waived with permission from the Barefoot Collective.

Nothing in this license impairs or restricts the authors' moral rights.

If You Give Me a Fish

you have fed me for a day.
If you teach me to fish
then you have fed me until
the river is contaminated or
the shoreline seized
for development.
But if you teach me
to organize
then whatever the challenge
I can join together
with my peers
And we will fashion
our own solution.

NORTHLAND POSTER COLLECTIVE   www.northlandposter.com   1-800-627-3082

CHAPTER ONE
Shaping our world

New ways of looking at organisations and social change

"We are best defined by the mystery"

We are greater than our despair.
The negative aspects of humanity
Are not the most real and authentic;
The most authentic thing about us
Is our capacity to create, to overcome,
To endure, to transform, to love,
And to be greater than our suffering.
We are best defined by the mystery
That we are still here, and can still rise
Upwards, still create better civilisations,
That we can face our raw realities,
And that we will survive
The greater despair
That the greater future might bring.

FROM "MENTAL FIGHT" BY BEN OKRI, 1999

HI THERE. I'M LOFTY...

Have you thought why organisations matter or what kind of organisations we need in the future? Does a "sovereign local organisation" sound interesting?
Is an organisation a machine or a living thing? And just how do organisations change? Are you a "cultural creative"?
If these questions are at all interesting, read on!

JAMES TELLS THIS STORY...

One of my favourite stories is about a group of rural women who were assisted by a development agency to start a vegetable garden in their community. The primary intention of the project was to improve the diets of community members. But its ultimate achievements went much further than this. In fact the women learnt so much and took so much courage from being part of the group that their ambitions grew as fruitfully as their seedlings. Before long they were producing more than their families could eat and selling the surplus. Respectfully presenting themselves to their chief, they petitioned for, and got, more land. Then they yanked a bunch of local men off their butts and paid them to fence their new land and build a shed for their tools. It didn't take long before their position in the community had changed as well. They had become a force to contend with. The women began involving others in their work and the project began to include widely divergent aspects of community life, both economic and political. In the end it was the success of their organisation rather than the vegetable garden itself that made the greatest impact on the community.

WHY ORGANISATIONS MATTER

Organisations matter. They make it possible for us to pool the strengths we have as individual human beings to achieve things that we could not do alone. They enable us to collectively mobilise our individual powers to face our human challenges with greater possibility.

But why do we put up with organisations that don't work, why do we tolerate tired old structures that make us unhappy and that worsen the very problems they are meant to solve? Why don't we pay more attention to the kinds of organisations we create? Particularly now, when it matters.

At this point in our history, humanity faces significant and urgent choices and decisions. The people making these choices and decisions are those who have the power of organisation behind them, be they governments with bureaucracies, be they businesspeople with corporate empires or be they ordinary people with local organisations and social movements behind them.

When ordinary people are able to create, link and strengthen their own organisations, and through them to voice and act out what they think, feel and want, they acquire more power over the choices and decisions that affect their lives. For those unnumbered millions living in poverty and without basic rights, organisation makes a different future possible.

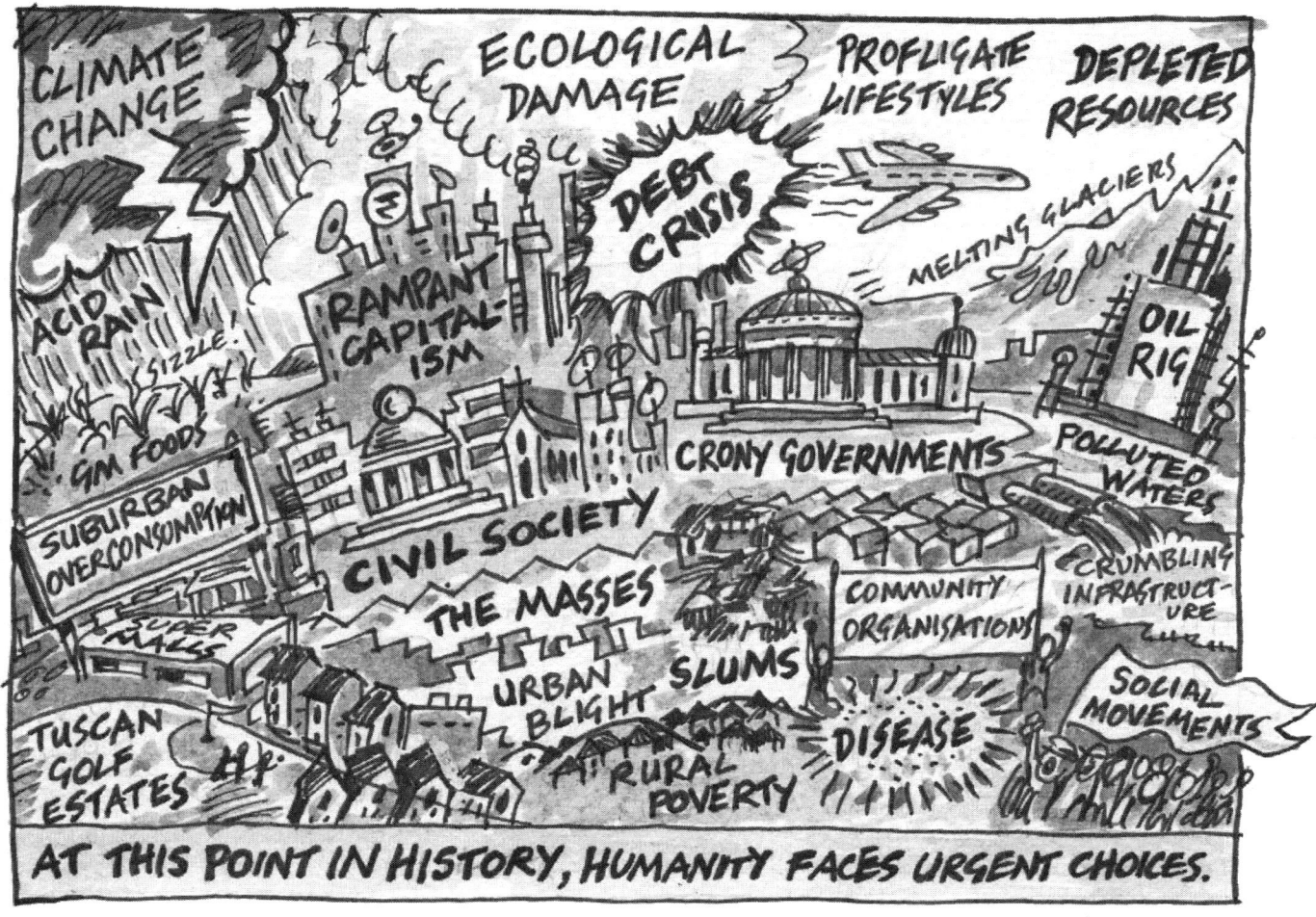

We may be tempted to see people's organisations and social movements as battering rams to knock down the walls of marginalisation and oppression and to claim their rights. And we may hope that by winning enough battles, we will win a war and usher in a new future. But while we must battle injustice whenever we find it, this is not enough. There is little evidence that seeing our challenges as a set of contests between oppressor and oppressed, between left and right or rich and poor, will render any gains we make permanent.

We may indeed win some battles and bring justice and relief, and we should do this where necessary. But it would be naive to think that the "war" against poverty, marginalisation and oppression will be finally won by only engaging in it as a war, as a fight. Indeed if we see this as a war we will forever be locked into a contest that is permanently stacked against our winning.

The economic power of the elites will always ensure that they will win at the contests they have defined and adapt the contest in their favour should they lose a battle or two. Worse still, a combat mentality may undermine our creativity for seeing new possibilities. We have to be wiser than this and look to the possibilities of deeper transformation.

> A combat mentality may undermine our creativity for seeing new possibilities.

CHAPTER ONE: SHAPING OUR WORLD

THE ZAPATISTAS OF MEXICO

SMALL FARMERS
AND FAIR TRADE NETWORKS

CITIZEN JOURNALISM
OPEN SOURCE NETWORKS
VIRTUAL COMMUNITIES
CREATIVE COMMONS

 FOR MORE RESOURCES DON'T FORGET OUR WEBSITE: www.barefootguide.org

REFUSING TO PLAY THE WAR GAME

The problem is not about whether to win the (war)game this way or that way, the problem is the game itself. In many ways we are all trapped in this game, rich and poor alike, in the thrall of a system that serves nobody's long-term interests. The game itself needs transforming, with an alternative thinking or logic, different principles and values, through transforming the people and organisations who play it and by experimenting with new forms of organisation, relationship and engagement between them.

> *You never change anything by fighting existing reality. To change something, build a new model that makes the existing model obsolete.*
>
> R. Buckminster Fuller

A NEW THINKING IS TAKING HOLD...

There are already signs that new thinking is taking hold. Consider...

The Zapatistas of Mexico, having laid down their arms and faced with the possibility of winning political power in Mexico in the 1990s, chose a different role, acknowledging that if they won and took power they would become like other parties, compromised and corrupt. Instead they have focused on transforming their relationship with the idea of government itself, beginning with changing the way they do things themselves. In the Chiapas region, they are re-creating government from below, autonomous and sovereign self-government, authentically theirs, an image of future possibilities.

Across the world small farmers are re-organising their relationships with each other and their customers, creating farmers' markets, decreasing their dependencies on agri-corporates through organic movements and fair trade networks. New forms of ethical community-based banking, like the Grameen banks or the daily savings schemes, are growing, enabling millions to access resources to invest in the future and building new forms of solidarity and community at the same time.

The internet is breaking the monopoly of the old media and communication elites, enabling surprising forms of networked organisation to emerge, not only in the North (Obama's ground campaign was an interesting example) but across the globe. Open source networks, creative commons, and virtual communities in social networking technologies linking people across the globe are beginning to redefine many relationships, especially amongst young people. Ideas are being exchanged, horizontally, at an extraordinary pace. Indeed, new models are already emerging.

CREATING SPACE FOR ALTERNATIVES

So new ground is being broken, not just by confronting the old hierarchies and taking over old levers of power, but also by creating space for offering and building alternatives. It is an emergent and experimental challenge to create new forms of organisation and networking and new forms of engagement between them, rather than continually recreating old forms of struggle. There will be many false starts and lessons learnt but something new is being stirred that is worth learning from.

"What kind of organisations does the future require?"

MOVING BEYOND CYNICISM

Many social activists have become cynical of approaches that are not centred on struggle and view some of these so-called innovations, like multi-stakeholder forums, as processes for subtle co-option, a trick. And they might be. But they don't have to be, particularly if they are grounded in strong grassroots organisation.

All of these innovations, if they are to make a meaningful and lasting difference to all people, must be founded on the active voices and engagement of ordinary people through their own sovereign, authentic and future-oriented local organisations. These are the building blocks of any future movement.

WHAT KIND OF ORGANISATIONS DOES THE FUTURE REQUIRE?

But again we must ask, and insist that this question keep being asked, what kind of organisations does the future require?

From all our experience we guess that the organisations of a future that works will be: more interdependent and participative, more humane, less hierarchical and competitive, freer of old discriminations, more networked and nimble and able to acknowledge the diverse strengths and real needs of their individual members, less tied to old dogmas and more able to learn from experience. We have started to witness organisations like this emerging and we believe that civil society has a key role to play in experimenting and innovating their forms.

> In the end the aggressors always destroy themselves, making way for others who know how to cooperate and get along. Life is much less a competitive struggle for survival than a triumph of cooperation and creativity.

Fritjof Capra

CHAPTER ONE: SHAPING OUR WORLD

Seeing what is there, supporting what is possible

"The fact that people, under the direst of circumstances, are able to pull themselves together and organise themselves is a celebration of the fact that the urge and impulse to develop and organise is inborn."

Local organisations begin small, often becoming more than originally intended, like the organisation of the women gardeners above. The fact that people, under the direst of circumstances, are able to pull themselves together and organise themselves is a celebration of the fact that the urge and impulse to develop and organise is inborn.

Support from the outside, from donors, NGOs, activists or government workers can help, but the will of people to develop their own organisations is an inborn fact that does not need to be imported, only unblocked and supported, if need be. Indeed attempts to import models of organisation from the outside (usually westernised managerial forms) have proven more likely to kill local attempts and fail for lack of ownership.

We can easily agree that locally owned organisation is a good thing, but will any kind of organisation do? How often have we seen good organisations, from community to global levels, torn apart through conflict, or wither away through poor leadership, or become destructive to their own people because of selfish and fearful egos, or die because they were unable to learn and adapt to changing circumstances? And how often have we found that the very things organisations are trying to change in the world exist right inside them? Many NGOs advocating a more equitable sharing of power in communities are themselves organised in traditional hierarchies.

Our task is not to help form or perpetuate organisations that exploit people or the natural environment in ways that exclude, deplete, diminish or disempower.

A SENSE OF SOVEREIGNTY

It has long been clear to us that in order for organisations or communities to change they need to have a strong sense of *sovereignty* in their decision-making and the way they relate to the world. This has been achieved in many small and often unnoticed ways as a result of the developmental work and support of many leaders and facilitators in civil society organisations, themselves members of communities dedicated to building healthy organisation. There are thousands upon thousands of civil society organisations that, despite enormous difficulties, have achieved high levels of sovereignty.

Seeing the future in sovereign local organisations

The word *sovereignty* is well-used by small-farmer organisations and allied practitioners when they speak of *food sovereignty* or *seed sovereignty* as a right to be self-reliant, of local ownership, of decision-making from a stance of consciousness and free-choice, not subject to the will and whims of those outside who may seek to control or exploit.

Sovereignty is a particularly powerful concept when applied to organisation, suggesting the same authentic qualities, describing a home-grown resilience, an inside-out identity, the idea of an organisation being the expression of the free will of its own constituents. It should be clear that rights like food sovereignty can only exist if they are embedded in strong, sovereign organisation.

> Sovereignty is both a quality of organisation to be developed and a right to be respected and defended. If development is about shifting or transforming power there has to be a clear concept of where power can be rightfully and sustainably held — sovereign local organisations and social movements are an obvious location.

SOVEREIGNTY IS NOT EASY

We witness vibrant, if disorganised, community-based organisations, movements and local NGOs, continuing to line up for funding, fitting themselves, their work, structure, language, indeed their life, into the templates of short-term funded projects and tightly contained project-cycles. Local organisations continue to be the service-providers of donors and government to achieve their externally formulated project goals, with a few participative processes thrown in to give them local flavour. And all gamely assisted by NGOs and professional consultants, themselves competing for funding and held to account against external measures. Sovereignty is a hard thing to do.

BEWARE OF LATTER-DAY MISSIONARIES

Some of the larger international NGOs working out of a rights-based approach have begun to recognise the importance of supporting local organisations and social movements as effective rights-holders. But despite the speak of "rights" we continue to witness local organisations or "partners" being assessed, even self-assessed, against templates, checklists and models of a "best practice" organisation developed in the North and having their capacity built accordingly.

CHAPTER ONE: SHAPING OUR WORLD

We witness lively volunteer-based organisations and emerging grassroots movements being rebuilt into more professional organisations losing their character and representing only those interests of the community that align with funding or NGO guidelines. We witness them developing into better-behaved citizens, possibly alleviating some small vestiges of poverty in the short-term, but angry only when the funding slows, no longer at the injustices they were born out of, becoming a pale shadow of their potential at best and a blockage to authentic development at worst. We sometimes wonder whether some NGOs and donors of the development sector have become latter-day missionaries, undermining indigenous potential and naively and unwittingly softening up the natives for more post-colonial globalisation!

This is development without local sovereignty and it has long accompanied the deepening poverty of the marginalised of this world. It is also extremely difficult for the development sector to admit this veiled role without exposing its own lack of sovereignty and backbone.

"There are sovereign organisations and movements on all continents bucking this trend, often supported by developmental donors and NGOs, and the sector needs to seek them out and learn from them."

THE SITUATION IS FAR FROM HOPELESS

The situation is far from hopeless. There are sovereign organisations and movements on all continents bucking this trend, often supported by developmental donors and NGOs, and the sector needs to seek them out and learn from them. There are many initiatives, programmes and projects that hold great promise if they can adjust or transform themselves towards incorporating a more directly organisational approach.

If this is true then it requires that development practitioners, including donors, pay more attention to the concept of organisation itself and the practice of facilitating the development of authentic and sovereign local organisation and social movements. There may be a growing body of professional OD facilitators in the sector, some of whom are developmental, but we believe that it is a discipline that needs to be more widely learnt and become more central to the practice of the sector as a whole, not just a small professional enclave.

Key aspects of sovereign organisations

What are some of the key aspects of the identity of a sovereign organisation or movement?

   ... such an organisation strives to know and work with its own purpose. It works on and out of clear principles and values and has the courage to hold onto these.

   ... it is an authentic expression of the will and voice of its own constituents. It can provide services but is not the service provider of another organisation's purpose, and while it may accept funding it is not a surrogate vehicle for the funded projects of outside agencies.

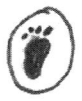   ... a sovereign organisation is culturally and structurally unique, not a clone of some external "best practice" template.

   ... a sovereign organisation is politically conscious, knows its rights and responsibilities and understands the power relationships it is held in.

   ... a sovereign organisation is able to cooperate and work with co-travellers and peers without losing its sense of self. Sovereignty does not denote parochial, insular behaviour, though there may be phases of independence, of inward development and of finding own identity, before opening up to collaboration.

   ... sovereignty is both a quality and a process of continual learning. The ability to learn and adapt will determine its sovereignty in a changing and volatile world and thus its increasing effectiveness. A sovereign organisation learns from many and varied sources, primarily its own hard-earned experience, but also through its diverse horizontal learning relationships with co-travellers and peers.

   ... a sovereign organisation is unlikely to meet the criteria of most donors.

FINDING THE REAL CHALLENGES OF DEVELOPMENTAL PRACTICE

It is in encouraging and supporting these qualities and processes that we may find the real challenges of developmental practice for NGOs and donors. What it requires is the time to see what is living in communities that is authentic, that has potential, accompanied by a deep respect for what is local and indigenous and a subtlety of practice to give thoughtful and careful support where it is needed.

It also requires facilitators and donors who are working on their own sovereignty, beholden to their own purposes and values, derived from the needs and rights of the people and organisations they seek to support.

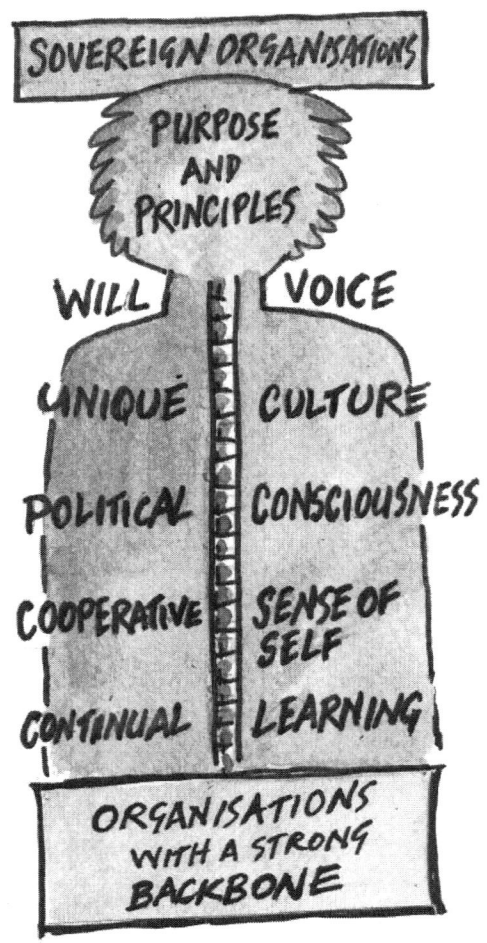

"What it requires is a deep respect for what is local and indigenous and a subtlety of practice to give thoughtful and careful support where it is needed."

Seeing the world through organisation

Community is an organisation made up of many other organisations, formal and informal, all ultimately based on a foundation of families, friendships and neighbourhoods. These are all organisations.

Communities themselves are parts of ever larger "organisations". These could be networks of civil society organisations, or social movements working locally or nationally or even global movements. Or we could see communities as the foundations of local municipalities which collectively form larger provincial governing structures going right through to nation states. Nation states are themselves a part of larger communities of nations, some regional and some global. The business world has its own organisational forms from local shops and markets to giant global corporations.

Human beings are social beings and we form organisations through which to be together and through which to do things together that we cannot do alone. Organisations are so much part of who we are, like the air that we breathe, that we can easily miss how significant they are to us. By bringing the needs, skills and abilities of individuals into relationship with each other in organisations, humankind has achieved almost unimaginable feats of creativity – but also of terrible destruction.

It is not only 'what' organisations do that changes the world. The kinds of organisations we create and the way we organise ourselves does so much to determine the nature and quality of human society. "We" are "organisations".

James Taylor

Seeing organisations: machines or living systems?

So many people see organisations as machines operated by humans – indeed it is probably the dominant idea of what an organisation is in the world today.

This mechanical view of organisations is comforting to managers who hope to control or drive their organisations in safe and predictable ways to known, planned destinations. Of course they can only do this by trying to force the people to behave like machine parts, obedient, predictable and unemotional. In doing so they squeeze out the creative sparks, the energising warmth and human spirit that enable healthy organisations to achieve what is possible, and to be sustainable into the future.

For us, organisations are messy, multifaceted, living systems, alive because they are populated by human beings in active relationships with the multiplied complexity of all individuals involved. Just as people need to be approached with more love, curiosity and wonder, to draw out the best in them, so too can organisations respond to a different kind of attention. What is it that distinguishes dull bureaucracy from vibrant and creative organisations?

Margaret Wheatley

LIVING SYSTEMS: WHAT MAKES THEM TICK?

It is when we see organisation as something other than its people, as other than human, that we reinforce all that lies at the bottom of what is wrong in the world: mechanical and inhuman organisations and behaviours that seek to control through systematic domination and exclusion.

If we see an organisation as a machine (consciously or not) then we might pay great attention to the visible things like its structure, its governance and decision-making procedures, the formal policies and the logical frameworks through which it is planned and organised.

Of course these more visible characteristics are important, but if we want to really understand what makes an organisation tick we might see it as a living system with these characteristics:

- The actual **values** and **principles** which guide the behaviours and actions of people in the organisation;
- The actual **practice** – not only what the plan says but what it actually does, its real work and the deeper thinking behind the doing;
- The human **relationships** between the people and between the organisation and the outside world;
- The **culture and habits** which describe the regular, unique and unwritten behaviours of each organisation;
- The organisation's **development** – the way it responds, learns, grows and changes over time. Unlike mechanical systems which degrade over time, living systems develop over time.

If we are interested in working with the life of the organisation it is in these areas that we will find it. By focusing only on the formal, more mechanical aspects, it is likely that we will reinforce what is not living and stifle what is. In paying more attention to these living aspects we are more likely to bring life and interest to the mechanical, so that they support rather than obstruct creative human agency.

A LIVING SYSTEMS APPROACH

A living systems approach helps us to see that these elements are dynamically and historically related, that health or dysfunction in any is rooted in the other, in virtuous and vicious cycles. So low organisational performance may have much to do with competitive, conflictual relationships and culture. This may be a product of a lack of investment in the development of the team, who in their confused state are trapped in working harder at a practice that no longer works, without the will or time to stand back and think about their challenges. It's a vicious cycle, like the woodcutter who has become too busy to sharpen his own axe.

> "When we see organisation as something other than its people, as other than human, we reinforce all that lies at the bottom of what is wrong in the world."

A living systems approach helps us to see that health or dysfunction in any is rooted in the other, in virtuous and vicious cycles.

CHAPTER ONE: SHAPING OUR WORLD

"So instead of trying to build "best practice" clones, we might rather ask "What is the real work of this organisation and what are the forms of organisation that best support this work?"

A living systems approach requires us to look for the more hidden and complex roots and cycles of organisational health and dysfunction rather than using the simplistic cause and effect mechanical thinking that dominates our world.

This world, inhabited by dynamic, living, changing systems, has developed an extraordinary diversity. Mechanical-minded managers try to "manage diversity" or even to minimise it with standard regulations and policies, rather than embrace its messiness and tensions. In so doing they kill the creativity that diversity has to offer.

"BEST PRACTICE" CLONES OR UNIQUE CREATIVITY

Given how complex living organisations are we must assume (and have experienced) that no two organisations are alike. So many of the most creative and successful organisations tend to break the rules of "best practice", finding their own unique ways of working suited to the kind of work they do and the kind of people they are. Recognising this diversity enables organisations to be themselves and in so being find their creativity, their best selves. So instead of trying to build "best practice" clones, we might rather ask "What is the real work of this organisation and what are the forms of organisation that best support this work?" Ironically, when we see a successful organisation we want to copy it, thus undermining the possibility of our own success based on our own uniqueness!

WWW.BAREFOOTGUIDE.ORG

KEY PRINCIPLES AND IDEAS GUIDING THIS BOOK

This book is guided by many principles and ideas, many learnt from others, but all honed and sharpened from experience. We offer four "guides" that we have found to be particularly true and useful in our work.

Development (and the will to develop) is a natural, inborn process.

In whichever state we may find organisations, they are already developing. They may or may not be developing healthily or in ways they like or are even conscious of, they may be stuck in some places, but they have been developing long before facilitators came into their lives and will continue to do so long after they have left. *We cannot deliver development* – it is already happening as a natural process that we need to read, respect and work with.

People's and organisation's own capacity to learn from experience is the foundation of their development, independence and interdependence.

Learning from experience is as old as the hills, one of the natural, organic processes, though seldom used consciously, by which people develop themselves. We learn by doing, by thinking about what we have done and then doing it a bit better next time. We also learn especially well from peers, horizontally, who share with us their experience, connecting it to our own experience.

Learning how to learn effectively, from own experience, enables people to take pride in their own intelligence and knowledge and to build a healthy independence from outside experts.

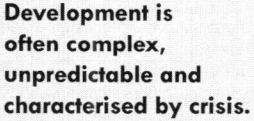

Development is often complex, unpredictable and characterised by crisis.

What does it take, and how long, to help a woman in crisis to find her courage to deal with an abusive husband or for a community to find the confidence to deal with corrupt councillors? When an organisation seems to be on the verge of imploding is this the end or a chance for renewal? What complex and unanticipated development of forces contributes to a once-flourishing social initiative rolling over and dying?

Development is inherently unpredictable and prone to crisis. Yet almost miraculously, developmental crises are pregnant with opportunities for new movement, for qualitative shifts.

Practitioners or donors often avoid offering support in times of crisis, thinking it signals failure, when the opposite may be possible. Recognising and working with crisis, with all its unpredictabilities, are central to a developmental approach.

Power is held and transformed in relationships.

We live, learn and develop within three kinds of relationships: relationship with self, interpersonal relationships with people around us and external relationships with the rest of the world. Power is held in relationships, whether it is the struggle we have with ourselves to claim our inner power, or the power some have over others or the power we hold with others, or the power the State wields in relation to its citizens – without relationship power means little, it has no force, for bad or for good. *If we want to shift power, we have to shift relationships.*

CHAPTER ONE: SHAPING OUR WORLD

Seeing the ways organisations change

KINDS OF CHANGE

EMERGENT CHANGE

TRANSFORMATIVE CHANGE

PROJECTABLE CHANGE

Living systems are constantly changing. Healthy change is what we need and seek and so we usually ask: "How do we change our organisation?" But it might be helpful to take a step back and first ask "How do organisations tend to change, how is this organisation already changing, whether visibly or not, and what conditions and possibilities for change exist?" Knowing how an organisation is changing, and what are its conditions of change, and embedding our work in those change processes already underway, is key to a developmental approach.

There are three major types of social change that we have observed that also apply to organisations.

EMERGENT CHANGE

Emergent change describes the day-to-day unfolding of life, where individuals, families, communities, organisations and societies change gradually and unconsciously, learning from experience, trial and error, trying to improve and enhance what they know and do, building on what is there, step-by-step, uncertainly, but still learning and adapting, however well or badly. It is change characterised by *action learning*.

TRANSFORMATIVE CHANGE

Organisations also get stuck or caught in crisis. When growth and complexity outstrip organisational capacity, when important needs are no longer being met, the organisation becomes unstable or out of balance and all sorts of unusual behaviours are let loose. The symptoms of this kind of change often show themselves in interpersonal conflict or more general organisational tension, growing towards crisis. Tension, conflict and power struggles are commonly experienced as negative and we try to avoid them. Yet situations of stuckness or crisis are often opportunities for significant, transformative change.

This kind of change happens mostly through difficult processes of *unlearning* the deeper attitudes, approaches, beliefs and values underlying the crisis and facing our fears, doubts and hatreds. Unlearning clears the way so that new, more appropriate foundations can be renewed or adopted.

PROJECTABLE CHANGE

When organisations are reasonably stable and healthy and when external conditions are not too unpredictable, then the conditions for projectable change exist. In such conditions people can often look far ahead, creating visions of what they want and making plans towards making them happen. Hence "Projects".

CREATING CONDITIONS FOR PROJECTABLE CHANGE

Many impoverished and marginalised communities (and their organisations) live in very unstable and unpredictable situations (of emergent or transformative change) where efforts to initiate inappropriate projectable change (projects) often fail, even if they are well-funded from the outside. External donors prefer projectable conditions (whether they exist or not) because they offer the promise, or illusion, of a safer outcomes-based investment. Because of this they often insist on projects where they are not yet possible. Indeed it often requires working through messy emergent or crisis-ridden transformative conditions in order to create the internal and external conditions for projectable change to flourish.

Seeing the future organisation of society

Nicanor Perlas, a Filipino activist, writes about the threefold nature of society. He sees society as being made up of the three interacting spheres, namely, civil society, government and business. He refers to this as the threefold nature of social life. He makes a case for the importance of the creative tension between these three subsystems for the healthy development of society. The creative forces in society come alive where the three come together in their attempts to shape each other. Society gets stuck when any one of the three becomes too dominant to the point where they are no longer fulfilling their unique purpose.

Perlas starts by describing the important functions of each of the three. He sees economic society e.g. business as dealing with "the production, distribution, and consumption of goods and services for the appropriate satisfaction of human needs". Its role is "to harness nature to efficiently meet human needs" through organising society to work together. Political society, largely government, is the "subsystem that deals with equality in all aspects of human relations".

Nicanor Perlas

CIVIL SOCIETY: THE "CULTURAL SPHERE"

Perlas views civil society as the "cultural sphere" of society and describes it as "that subsystem of society concerned with the development of full human capacities and the generation of knowledge, meaning, art, ethics, and a sense of the sacred. Culture is the realm that gives identity and meaning, that represents the deeper voice of community. This is the realm that develops the full human potential of individuals and organisations and enables them to be competent participants in the economy, political life, culture, and society at large." Civil society, as the people and organisations, thus plays a unique and deeply humanising role in the development of society.

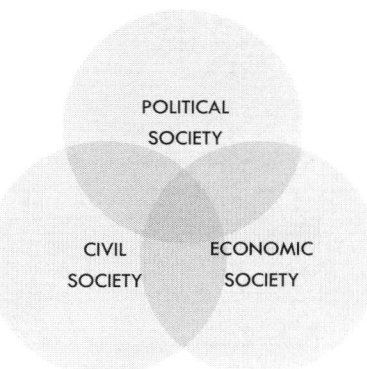

CHAPTER ONE: SHAPING OUR WORLD

> "The future of a just, healthy and free society will require the transformation of the organisation of all sectors of society."

FOR MORE RESOURCES DON'T FORGET OUR WEBSITE:
www.barefootguide.org

CULTURAL CREATIVES

Perlas recognises that there are individuals in civil society, government and business, working towards changing their worlds through the values of civil society – he calls them "cultural creatives". It is likely that these cultural creatives, as leaders and facilitators, will help to connect the world to new organisational forms.

The future of a just, healthy and free society will require the transformation of the organisation of all sectors of society: of government from its self-serving bureaucracy to an organisation that fearlessly protects its citizens, ensuring equality and justice; of business from its short-term obsession with quarterly returns to being longer-term investors in sustainable livelihoods; and of civil society from its combative victimhood to its cultural role of expanding freedom for individuals, community and society alike.

In each case these roles will require new forms of organisations, living systems, that really enable us to collectively mobilise our individual powers to face our human challenges with greater possibility.

CULTURAL CREATIVES HELP TRANSFORM SOCIETY

CHAPTER TWO
Inside Out

Towards understanding ourselves, other people and how we change

HOWZIT, MY NAME IS KAMA...

But this chapter is about you. If you are going to help others to better understand themselves, you might want to begin by better understanding yourself. We will look at how, as a leader or facilitator, you can ask better questions and how you can be more facilitative. We will introduce a variety of 'windows' through which you can better see yourself and others. My guess is that you will enjoy the experience. You may also find that you are a lot more interesting than you thought you were! Enjoy!

LOFTY TELLS THIS STORY...

Several years ago a colleague offered me some wonderfully simple advice. "If you want to know what is really happening inside an organisation or group that you're working with," she said, "you should pay more attention to what is happening inside you. Your own feelings often provide the most important clues."

What she was pointing to, I think, is that our hearts are also sense organs. Through our feelings, our gut feel or intuition, we are able to hear at a deeper level. But learning to listen to and trust your own feelings isn't easy. I was brought up to be suspicious of feelings – they're not logical, I was told, and therefore not to be trusted. Unlearning deep-seated attitudes like this isn't easy. I've still got a long way to go, but my friend's advice provided me with a new window through which to see the world. Being more in touch with my feelings and intuition has certainly helped me to feel more alive.

If you want to be an effective leader or facilitator, you've first got to hold a mirror up to yourself.

WALKING THE TALK

If our aim as leaders, practitioners or facilitators is to help others to see and hear themselves and each other more clearly, we first need to be in touch with our own thoughts, feelings and desires. If we really want to see and hear the people we're working with, we need to practise on ourselves first – to walk our own talk.

ASKING GOOD QUESTIONS

It's not just what you ask,
It's also who you ask.

WHY DO WE NEED GOOD QUESTIONS?

One of the signs of a facilitative leader is the ability to ask the right questions at the right time. The art of leadership depends on the ability to ask questions that will make a difference.

This ability depends in turn on the ability to listen effectively. It's not hard to see that questioning and listening skills go well together. Really listening to people helps us to ask good questions. And if we ask good questions then we are more likely to get responses that are worth listening to!

As practitioners or leaders, the questioning process begins with us. But the ultimate objective is to help people to listen to the world more deeply and ask their own good questions about it. This lies at the heart of empowerment.

ENDA MOCLAIR, A DEVELOPMENT PRACTITIONER IN CAMBODIA, TELLS THIS STORY...

Before each meeting with partners we would develop different scenarios and questions, select suitable metaphors and common experiences and link to local lore. We would think about all those attending, put ourselves in different shoes and try empathising with their experiences and background: 'Who were they? What was their story? What had their life experiences to date been? How might this colour or influence the way they perceive their situation, how might our own responses influence their responses?' In this light we would re-evaluate our questions and try and mould questions which would encourage conversation.

Effective questions

According to Irene Leonard, asking effective questions is the easiest way to get the right answers. It seems simple but is a point that is often overlooked. Effective questions, she says, are powerful and thought provoking, without being too aggressive. They are questions that ask "what?" or "how?" and not always "why?". "Why" questions, she warns, are good for soliciting information but may make people defensive. Another key trick to asking effective questions is to wait for the answer more patiently, giving people more space to be thoughtful.

"When you are working together with other people to solve a problem," says Leonard, "it is not enough to tell them what the problem is; they need to find out what the problem is themselves. You can help them do this by asking them thought-provoking questions." Rather than making assumptions about what you think the other person may know, you might ask: *"What do you think the problem is?"*

Effective questioning is useless if you do not have the ability to listen and suspend judgment. This means being intent on understanding what the person who is talking is *really* saying, or what they are *trying* to say. What is the meaning behind their words? Let go of your own opinions so that they do not block your understanding and learning of important information, and pay attention to your gut or instinct for additional information.

> "Behind effective questioning lies the ability to listen and suspend judgment."

EXERCISE

Asking better questions

This exercise contains a very simple but powerful action learning tool. It uses a question-driven approach to change, by helping participants to find a question that matters. Participants are encouraged to reflect on the experience that gave rise to their question, and then to improve, deepen or rethink their question. They are then asked to say what they will do next towards finding an answer to the question. The exercise does not push participants to find quick or simple answers to their questions, but helps them take the next step in their own questioning process.

The exercise can be adapted to many situations and can be conducted with individuals or collectively. In this version, participants work in pairs.

1. COLLECTING YOUR QUESTIONS – CHOOSING ONE THAT MATTERS

Spend a few minutes thinking of and writing down a few burning questions you are facing in your practice or in your life. Make sure that you are in the question – like "How can I gain deeper trust of the organisation?" It should not be a question that somebody else should be asking– like "Why doesn't the government provide better support to small farmers?"

Choose one of your questions and think about how you have worded it. Write down the feelings that you have that accompany this question.

2. SURFACING THE EXPERIENCE BEHIND THE QUESTION

Where does this question actually come from? Try to recall an experience (or two) which led you to this question… take yourself back into the experience. Write down any important memories or observations. What feelings accompany this story?

3. SHARE WITH A PARTNER

Tell your question and story to your partner (who is listening with curiosity!). After this the partner should say what struck them about the story and question, and then suggest what they think was really happening – the real story behind the story. What advice do they have for your question?

4. RETHINK YOUR ORIGINAL QUESTION

Now try to improve your question. Perhaps a better question comes to mind.

Write it down. Also write down the feelings that accompany this new or improved question.

5. WHAT WILL YOU DO NEXT?

Write down your next step towards answering your question.

6. SHARE WITH THE GROUP

If working in a larger group, it may help to share all the questions and accompanying feelings. Sharing deep questions can promote healthy conversations.

GOOD FACILITATION AND FACILITATIVE LEADERSHIP

SOME PRINCIPLES

A great question to ask in organisational and community development processes is:

"Who is participating in whose process?"

- As leaders and facilitators we understand that people are already developing along their own journeys. Our role is to help them see their journey and the countryside more clearly so that they can make their own choices. We are participating in their process!

- We have deep respect and curiosity for who people are, what they know, what we see of them and even what we do not yet see. (There is always more than meets the eye.)

- We are interested in and listen deeply to what people think, what they feel and what they want.

- We help people to surface their own hidden knowledge and resourcefulness, and to appreciate and celebrate their own power.

- We help people ask their own questions, form their own judgements and make their own choices, even if we disagree.

- We help people learn from their own and each other's experiences. More importantly, we help them to learn how to learn effectively so that they can become more independent thinkers.

- We work for the good of the whole community or organisation, not the interests of the few.

"As leaders and facilitators we understand that people are already developing along their own journeys."

A STORY

Rafting

Tony Watkins

This story is an excellent illustration of the difference between commanding leadership and facilitative leadership.

By good fortune I was able to raft down the Motu River twice during the last year. The magnificent four-day journey traverses one of the last wilderness areas on the North Island.

The first expedition was led by 'Buzz', an American guide with a great deal of rafting experience and many stories to tell of mighty rivers such as the Colorado. With a leader like Buzz there was no reason to fear any of the great rapids on the Motu.

The first half day, in the gentle upper reaches, was spent developing teamwork and co-ordination. Strokes had to be mastered, and the discipline of following commands without question was essential. In the boiling fury of a rapid there would be no room for any mistake: when Buzz bellowed above the roar of the water an instant reaction was essential.

We mastered the Motu. In every rapid we fought against the river and we overcame it. The screamed commands of Buzz were matched only by the fury of our paddles, as we took the raft exactly where Buzz wanted it to go.

At the end of the journey there was a great feeling of triumph. We had won. We proved that we were superior. We knew that we could do it. We felt powerful and good. The mystery and the majesty of the Motu had been overcome.

The second time I went down the Motu the experience I had gained should have been invaluable, but the guide was a soft-spoken Kiwi. It seemed that it would not even be possible to hear his voice above the rapids.

As we approached the first rapid, he never even raised his voice. He did not attempt to take command of us or the river. Gently and quietly he felt the mood of the river and watched every little whirlpool. There was no drama and no shouting. There was no contest to be won. He loved the river.

We swept through each rapid with grace and beauty, and after a day the river had become our friend, not an enemy. The quiet Kiwi was not our leader, but only the person whose sensitivity was more developed than our own. Laughter replaced the tension of achievement.

Soon the quiet Kiwi was able to lean back and let us take turns as leader. A quiet nod was enough to draw attention to the things our lack of experience prevented us from seeing. If we made a mistake then we laughed and it was the next person's turn.

We began to penetrate the mysteries of the Motu. Now, like the quiet Kiwi, we listened to the river and we looked carefully for all those things we had not even noticed the first time.

At the end of the journey we had overcome nothing but ourselves. We did not want to leave behind our friend the river. There was no contest, and so nothing had been won. Rather, we had become one with the river.

THE FOUR WINDOWS

There are dozens of different ways to better understand ourselves — it's a bit like looking through the different windows of a house. Each window gives us a different point of view. In this chapter we look through four 'windows' designed to help us to look at ourselves as individuals, as members of community, and as human beings.

 FOR MORE RESOURCES DON'T FORGET OUR WEBSITE: www.barefootguide.org

MODELS AND METAPHORS FOR UNDERSTANDING OURSELVES

In this chapter we explore four models for looking at the human individual:

- The Three-fold Human Being;
- Phases of Individual Development;
- The Four Temperaments; and
- Leadership Polarities.

Like the many other models used in this book, these 'windows' have arisen out of decades of social process work conducted by development practitioners all over the world. Where possible, we have tried to give some idea of the origins of these models, the key thinkers behind them, and where to look for more information about them.

ND GIVES SOME BACKGROUND...

By our very nature human beings are complex creatures, and understanding ourselves and each other has been a favourite — and very necessary — pastime since the year dot. Over the centuries we have evolved metaphors, models and systems of belief that help us better understand ourselves and our place in the world.

One of the oldest systems for understanding human beings is based on the idea that we are comprised of three major aspects: Mind, Body and Spirit. Despite all the advances of modern science and technology, this system of belief is still in place. It is common to most of the world's religions, and also informs many other branches of human knowledge.

While Eastern religious traditions have tended to emphasise the integration of mind, body and spirit, Western traditions have tended to think of them as being separate. The Newtonian or 'positivist' scientific tradition, named after Sir Isaac Newton (1643-1727), has generally avoided talking about spirit at all. Steering clear of those aspects of life that can't be empirically proved through scientific observation, Western scientists have preferred to leave all the spiritual stuff for the Church to deal with.

Today we have access to scientific models that clearly demonstrate that the Newtonian system was deeply flawed. Today's new models, based on quantum physics, systems theory, deep ecology and other advanced systems of thought, work with the realisation that everything is interconnected and that it is impossible to look at anything in isolation. This way of thinking about the world has been a characteristic of Eastern philosophy and religion for thousands of years. As the world changes, the dominance of the positivistic scientific traditions is receding, and more integrated models that combine the best of Western and Eastern systems of thought are evolving.

THE FIRST WINDOW

THE THREE-FOLD HUMAN BEING

Listening to the head, heart and feet

Listening and Questioning are without doubt the two most important skills. It's amazing, but if we are able to listen deeply to people, ask really good questions, and get people to do the same, our job is more than halfway done.

So, this is a very practical window. Think of it as a model for listening to people. Are you able to listen 'between the lines'? Can you hear the subtext beneath the main text? Can you hear, not just what people are saying, but what they are trying to say? Are you able to connect with what they are really feeling, and not just what they say they're feeling? Is it possible for you to ascertain what it is that they really want?

We call this deeper listening. It is one of the most important skills of a leader, development practitioner or facilitator.

LISTENING AT 3 LEVELS... TOGETHER!

We tend to place a heavy emphasis on thinking and rational thought without realising that our decisions in life come from the powerful combination of thinking, feeling and willing.

More often than not, what we think, what we feel and what we want are different things. Sometimes they can even be opposed. The challenge is to pay attention not only to logic and common sense, but also to the powerful messages delivered by the emotions and by the will.

LOFTY SHARES THIS SCENARIO...

Imagine that I'm a senior staff member and you're a new staff member. I ask you to sit with me and reflect on your work. You say "Ok, fine!" — it seems a good idea at first — but then you become anxious. You've had bad experiences of these kinds of interactions in the past. So although it sounds like a good idea, deep down you don't want to do it. Your rational mind and your will are at odds with one another. You may not even be conscious of this. Once we sit down together, all kinds of emotions kick in, you come across to me as defensive, and I start to worry about your work. Meanwhile, the reality is that your work is fine.

The trick is to listen not only to your logical response, but also to your feelings and will. As the senior staff member, I should be sensitive to your anxieties, and ask you how you feel about reflecting on your work with me. In listening to your answer, I should look for clues about your true feelings, not just what you say.

Head, heart and feet

We are THINKING human beings — we think about the things we perceive in order to understand them.

We are FEELING human beings — we experience the world through our emotions.

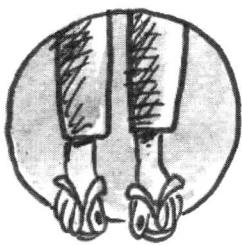

We are WILLING human beings — our needs and desires motivate us to act.

CHAPTER TWO: INSIDE OUT

LISTENING TO OUR HEADS, HEARTS AND FEET... TOGETHER

LISTENING TO THE HEAD

This is the thinking level, made up of perceptions, thoughts, facts, concepts, arguments, ideas and spiritual insights.

Listening non-judgementally means being open-minded and genuinely interested in where the other person is coming from, how they think and what assumptions they make.

LISTENING TO THE HEART

This is the feeling level, made up of emotions, moods and non-verbal experiences. Listening for feelings, paying attention to tone of voice, facial expressions, eyes and gestures. Empathetic listening means putting yourself in the other person's shoes. Listening to the silences can reveal feelings of disagreement or inadequacy, boredom or anger.

LISTENING TO THE FEET

This is the will level, where you listen for what people really want. Often, speakers themselves are only dimly aware of their own intentions and desires. It's surprising how few people are fully aware what motivates them and what they actually want in a situation. Skilful listening uncovers what lies 'behind' their thoughts and 'below' their feelings. Body language can reveal the will — a strong body presence may demonstrate a strong will, while a withdrawn body may reveal a weak will.

ESSENTIAL CHALLENGES OF LISTENING AT 3 LEVELS

 People all have their own ways of seeing the world and thinking about things. Be careful not to assume they see things the way you do.

 Listening to someone's true feelings gives you important clues about what really matters to them.

 The will level is where resistance to change usually resides. Helping people to listen to and transform their own will is one of the deepest challenges of change.

Some challenges of deeper listening

QUIETEN YOUR MIND...

Given the amount of stuff going on in our own heads, it's amazing that we can even follow what other people are saying. Following the thoughts of a speaker is actually not such an easy thing to do. It requires us to put our own thoughts, feelings and will on hold for the moment. Once we do that, we are better able to hear what is really being said.

LISTENING TO ALL THREE LEVELS... TOGETHER

Try and work out whether what the person is saying truly reflects what they think, what they feel or what they want, and whether these are similar or different. It's not easy to separate these three components, and involves skillful listening.

FOLLOWING FEELINGS

The surface thoughts that people express can be quite misleading. That's why listening for someone's true feelings is necessary if we want to discover what really matters to them. If we can't identify their real feelings, it's going to be difficult to really understand why they are thinking in a particular way, or what they really want. Many people are out of touch with their own feelings and so a lot of our work involves helping people to access and describe them.

A good way to start is to simply ask people about their feelings. Encouraging them to express the range of feelings they are experiencing – especially their mixed feelings – can be very revealing.

Many people lack a vocabulary of different feelings. How can you help them build their vocabulary but without suggesting to them what they are feeling?

As humans we are capable of holding mixed, and often contradictory, feelings. We all have our love/hate relationships. I can be happy to see you but upset that you are late, both at the same time. Surfacing mixed feelings can help us understand why people behave the way they do, often in such confusing ways!

DON'T PRESSURISE!

People who struggle to express their feelings should not be pressurised to do so in public. Traumatic experiences in their lives may have led them to push their feelings away, to protect themselves from reliving the past. Some people will only reveal their true feelings in a one-on-one relationship with a person they trust.

THE IMPATIENCE TRAP

If we are listening to someone, we often "get" what they are saying before they are finished. Waiting for someone to battle through a long explanation of what seems to be an obvious point can be quite tiresome. Common responses are either to cut them short, or to tune out and think about something else while waiting for them to finish. But as facilitators we

---

A fun Exercise

In pairs, face each other and tell each other what you did yesterday... but **you must both speak at the same time!** Do this for a minute.

Now discuss what happened and then ask yourselves how often you end up doing this kind of thing in everyday life without even realising it.

SOME PRACTICAL IDEAS

Here's how to get people in touch with their own thoughts and feelings before they participate in a discussion:

* Before a group discussion give participants a few minutes to think about the topic on their own, so that they can get in touch with their own thoughts and feelings about it.

* Suggest that they chat briefly to the person next to them to try out their ideas. This generally leads to greater participation.

* Where appropriate encourage people to express their feelings and what they want, not just their thoughts.

* **A Word of Caution:** Some people, when asked what they feel, say "I feel that...". This will always be a thought, not a feeling.

* Journaling is a great technique to get people to focus. Give participants a chance to sit quietly and write down their ideas, feelings and wants, and to think of questions that matter to them.

The Paralysis of Will

Why we don't act on our thoughts and feelings?

I FEEL TOTALLY PARALYSED
WILL

Often we feel powerless because we know we need to change but can't. Something stops us. We are experiencing a paralysis of will.

Usually this results from:

Doubt or self-doubt:

We doubt if people or situations can really change for the better. We doubt our own ability to meet the challenges of the future.

Hatred or self-hatred:

We resent or even hate others for past hurts. We hate ourselves for what we have done.

Fear:

We fear letting go of what we know even if it doesn't work. We fear the unknown ahead of us.

Transformation may require that we surface these doubts, hatreds and fears, so that we can deal with them.

---

should be careful not to fall into the impatience trap. We need to keep listening, consciously, for the feelings behind the thinking, and for the will being expressed by the speaker. This is deeper listening.

WAYS OF THINKING

What this all points to is that people have their own ways of thinking, their own meanings for words, and draw upon different experiences from ours to make meaning.

If we don't allow for differences in the other person's frame of reference, we're likely to get our wires crossed when talking to them. Worse, we sometimes assume we know what they're talking about when we don't.

We've all heard someone say "I know just what you mean". And we've all watched these know-it-all's demonstrate that they don't have a clue what we mean. We should be careful not to do the same thing.

Assuming everyone thinks alike is a major source of confusion.

❸ CHALLENGES:

KNOW THYSELF • EXPRESS THYSELF • ACT OUT OF THYSELF

Martin Buber

> *There are three principles in a man's being and life, the principle of thought, the principle of speech, and the principle of action. The origin of all conflict between me and my fellow-men is that I do not say what I mean and I don't do what I say.*

❶ KNOW YOURSELF
Think more of your own thoughts! Ask more of your own questions! Get in touch with your own feelings! Find out more of what you want!

❷ EXPRESS YOURSELF
Knowing what you think, feel and want makes it easier to express yourself and to stand up for yourself!

❸ ACT OUT OF YOURSELF
Act out of your own thoughts, your feelings and your will! Be yourself! Do what you must do! Have courage!

THE SECOND WINDOW

PHASES OF INDIVIDUAL DEVELOPMENT
Understanding the life-story of an individual

"Storytelling is at the heart of development work"

LOFTY TELLS THIS STORY...

Ten years ago I went on a four day Biography Workshop in Cape Town. We were required to look back over our lives and re-live key experiences through storytelling. I found myself examining my own life story as if I was studying a novel, or someone else's biography. I thought hard about the relationships with others that had made up my life, and then tried to imagine my own future story, looking at where I wanted my life to go.

Looking at my own past, present and future like this was both a painful and joyous experience. It gave me the most complete picture of myself that I had ever had. I left the workshop feeling bigger inside, with deeper roots into the past and a new appreciation of what I was capable of in the future.

I think this was when I realised that storytelling lies at the heart of development work. Storytelling is a practice that helps people to become conscious of their own stories, their own past, present and future, so that they can take hold of their own stories and begin to create the future that they want.

Once I was alerted to biography work, I began to notice how many development practitioners use it. I've been told about the effectiveness of this technique, for example, by practitioners working with abused women in the slums of Mexico City, or with young men in cultural programmes in Khayelitsha in Cape Town, or with small-holder farmers in Masvingo in Zimbabwe. The common thread in all these accounts is the use of storytelling to help people re-construct (in a sense, re-author) their own and their communities' life stories. In the process of re-authoring, people come to appreciate the richness of their own histories and the relevance of their own local knowledge.

MY LIFE AS A BOOK

One of the sessions in the Biography Workshop was, through writing and drawing exercises, to re-author our lives as though each of us was the subject of a book. We had to divide our lives into chapters and thread the narrative through them, bringing the story up to the present. Then we had to try and imagine our next chapter.

By looking at my life as a book I was able to see patterns in my behaviour across the chapters of my life. For example, I noticed that I had often felt disempowered in the company of older men. There had been a number of occasions where I resorted to immature or rebellious behaviour when I felt challenged by or disagreed with older men. I was now able to see how these challenges could have been dealt with more effectively. Seeing the patterns of my own behaviour was a huge help. It enabled me to recognise and anticipate these responses in order to make different choices in the future.

There are things in my past that I'm not proud of, and some deep regrets that are still a burden to me. Biographical work has helped me to forgive myself and let go of the burdens I carried. It's also helped me to forgive others, thus releasing some of the hurt and bitterness that was dragging me down.

At the same time, I was able to see all the good stuff I've done in my life. By recognising my own achievements I was able to gain a new appreciation of my own strengths.

Each of us uses the lessons from life differently. There is no better way to see this than in the lives of elderly people. Some seem locked in the past, continually moaning about lost opportunities. Others, despite their age, are still excited about life's challenges. To me, these people seem immensely wise. They stand out as big individuals.

Obviously, examining your past life like this is not an easy thing to do. Doing it in a facilitated workshop situation is so much easier that trying to do it on your own. The tendency to edit out all the stuff we don't want to remember is just too great. That's why storytelling requires an audience, even if it's just an audience of one. Sharing your story with someone you trust is where storytelling begins.

And, clearly, as a leader or facilitator it is important to have struggled with your own story before you begin to help other people work with their stories.

3 ARCHETYPAL PHASES

These phases are not only found in Western thinking, but appear to be an archetype common to many cultures.

DEPENDENCY

The *dependent* phase from lasts from birth to the early 20s.

INDEPENDENCE

The *independent* phase lasts from our 20s to our 40s.

INTERDEPENDENCE

The *interdependent* phase often kicks in at middle age, but can arrive much earlier.

Phases of human development

No individual is born complete or fully developed. Throughout life we continue to learn and grow, although what we learn is often dictated by what stage of life we are at. This process can be seen as continuous, while at the same time moving through stages or phases. Although each individual life path is different, human life has certain common phases.

There have been many interpretations of these phases, and one can find many different models of human development in modern developmental psychology. These models go back to the theoretical foundations laid by Aristotle and other classical scholars, which were subsequently elaborated during the 18th century by Descartes and other Enlightenment philosophers. In the 20th century, Freud outlined five stages of psychosexual development and Rudolf Steiner described 10 stages of development throughout human life. Whatever model one chooses, however, it becomes clear that these are all variations of the archetypal model in terms of which human life is divided into three phases: Childhood, Adulthood and Old Age. In terms of our relationships with each other, these phases are characterised by three states of being: **Dependence, Independence and Interdependence**. These phases are not only found in Western thinking, but appear to be an archetype common to many cultures. For example, ancient Chinese teachings reflects similar phases, known as a time to learn, a time to fight and a time to grow wise.

In terms of the model, the dependent phase lasts from conception until we are able to make our own way in life – usually in our early 20s. The independent phase arises when, as young adults, we question or reject the 'givens' that we grew up with, strive to formulate our own ideas and become financially self-sufficient. This phase can last into the mid-40s. The interdependent phase arises when there is a mature recognition that to achieve life's full potential we need to cooperate actively with other people in order to give back something to the world. This phase often kicks in at middle age, but can arrive much earlier.

Ten phases of individual development

According to Bernard Lievegoed, the three major phases of life can further be divided into ten phases, each seven years long. The problem with Lievegoed's formulation is that while everyone seems to agree on the existence of the three main phases, the age groups that apply to these stages may vary from one culture or society to another. For example, in countries where the average life expectancy is shorter due to the prevalence of infectious diseases, fewer people are likely to reach the age of 63 that, according to Steiner, signals the onset of the phase he called "Free Time". Similarly, in societies such as our own, where, because of AIDS deaths or other factors, children find themselves with the responsibilities of caring for an entire household while still in their teens, the transition from childhood to adulthood may be accelerated, and very traumatic.

For this reason we have adapted Steiner's model to make it more flexible, retaining his suggested ten phases without aligning them to specific age groups.

Ten phases of development

DEPENDENCY

1. THE PHASE OF IMITATION

- When a child is born it is completely dependent on its parents for basic human needs; food, shelter and warmth, as well as the emotional needs of love and trust.
- Children learn primarily through imitation and role modeling, therefore play is immensely important at an early age. It allows the infant an opportunity to mimic and copy the human behavior they see around them. Mother and father figures are the first models for children to learn the balance between masculine and feminine in each of them.
- Children learn to use language at an early age, building up sixty percent of their vocabulary in this period.
- Children have very fertile imaginations and in this period they cannot always distinguish between fantasy and reality.
- At this stage it is important that a child develops self confidence and a good concept of their self and their ability.

... from 0 to ±20 years

2. TESTING AUTHORITY

- The world outside becomes increasingly important at this stage (for example, schools, teachers and friends, which the child will integrate into his/her world view.
- Other role models besides the parents will emerge, such as teachers and friends.
- Children may start to contest authority, particularly of their parents. This too can be seen as a learning process.
- Children may start to articulate their thinking, particularly around issues like: good and evil, competition, beauty and ugliness, truth and untruth and fantasy and reality. They will often develop a sense of their own values in this period.
- At this stage children are often ready to take on some responsibility.

3. "WHO AM I?"

- Puberty can be seen as a time when a person searches for their own individuality and identity in the world, often defying and exploring the notions of authority in this search.
- It is a time for growth of sexual awareness and the questioning of sexuality. It is the onset of woman/manhood that is signified by physical changes such as menstruation in girls and the boys' voices cracking and getting deeper.
- Ideals and idols become important, such as pop singers and film stars. There is often a strong identification with a certain group or hero/heroine.
- It can be a period of intense emotions such as insecurity, loneliness, boredom and anger. These are sometimes related to the search 'for the meaning of life' that the young teenager may be going through.

CHAPTER TWO: INSIDE OUT

Ten phases of development (contd.)

INDEPENDENCE

±18 to 45 years

4 A TIME FOR CREATIVITY

- This can be seen as an explorative phase, when the young adult wants to have as many new experiences as possible. It is a search for sensations, experimentation with borders and limits, a time of wandering and traveling, but also of childbearing and raising. The young adult may change jobs, or even places they live in many times in this period.
- It is a time of increased independence, when one's own space and lifestyle choices become important, sometimes distancing the young adult from his/her family
- The notion and fear of conformity become prevalent in some cases, as the young adult wants to make a life for themselves that is different and exciting.

5 "MY OWN PHILOSOPHY"

- This is a time when there is a tendency towards specialisation and a readiness to deepen understanding.
- As an adult there is more creative ability accessible to respond to different situations.
- It is a time when people may have found their place in the world and are using it to their advantage. A settling down phase.
- There are dangers to be faced here, such as becoming stuck in a certain routine and not accessing new creative energy.

6 THE MIDDLE PASSAGE

- This period can be described as almost a "second puberty" that brings up a deep questioning of personal identity.
- It is a period where self doubt is common, as your assumptions of life are challenged by experience.
- The recognition that many things you wanted to do are not yet completed can be difficult to accept, along with the first signs of physical decline; the inevitability of getting older and the fact that you will die at some stage.
- It can be a painful and emotional period. Some people respond by indulging in escapist behavior such as: alcohol abuse, workaholism or expensive hobbies.

WWW.BAREFOOTGUIDE.ORG

Ten phases of development (contd.)

INTERDEPENDENCE

±40 years to...

7. THE PIONEERING STAGE

- Emergence from the crisis with new values and meaning can be an uplifting experience. At this point some people make radical life changes; new jobs or careers and approaching things with new attitudes.
- Moments in life are more appreciated through a new attitude.
- A new-found freedom may bring new interests and strengths.
- One may find an enhanced ability to bring "inner" and "outer" worlds together, while incorporating the views of others.
- A sense of real self knowledge is brought about by the experience of life.

8. A TIME FOR WISDOM

- A tranquil time in which a new respect for nature is developed. It is a time when you may discover your own uniqueness.
- There is the danger of contemptuous talk and behaviour if a person has not come to grips with the slipping away of youth at this stage. A respect should develop for the task of youth in life.
- A sense of wisdom that is rooted in experience, self knowledge and knowledge of the world may develop
- An interest in long term development may arise.

9. A TIME FOR REVIEW

- Issues that have not been fully dealt with earlier in life may come back with a vengeance.
- There may be the realisation that the work of life is not finished and there is little time to put things right.
- It is a time for dealing with the negatives of one's own personality.
- The fear of becoming too old to look after oneself; having to become dependent on others might be painful.
- A heightened awareness of death and coming to terms with it.

10. FREE TIME

- In these late years time becomes "free" if we decide we are responsible and have the capacity to truly love. If not we will be needy but unable to give unconditional love.
- There is an important choice to be made; one can choose to hang onto things from the past or let go and gracefully give and accept love.
- The retrospective perception of life; one can appreciate that although people are imperfect, mostly they genuinely strive for something better. This is true respect for the individual.

CHAPTER TWO: INSIDE OUT

THE THIRD WINDOW

THE FOUR TEMPERAMENTS
Finding our inner fire, air, water and earth

From the basic elements of Fire, Air, Water and Earth come four basic human temperaments.

FIRE
People with a fiery temperament often behave in a fiery way. Passionate, forceful, quick to anger, quick to forgive, they are often eager to take on leadership positions.

WATER
People with a watery temperament are calm and relaxed, low-key, easygoing and patient – if a bit slow for others.

AIR
Cheerful, positive, talkative and optimistic, people of an airy temperament love to juggle tasks, but sometimes drop the ball.

EARTH
Cautious, serious, sensitive and critical, people with an earthy temperament can be overly critical of self and others.

Introduction

The model of the Four Temperaments has been around for a long time. Its origins go back to ancient Egypt or Mesopotamia, but it was not formalised until around 400BC when it was linked by ancient Greek physicians to the theory of the Four Elements: Earth, Water, Air and Fire. Hippocrates developed this linkage into the theory of the Four Humours. He believed that some human behaviours were caused by bodily fluids (which he called "humours"). The four humours are blood, (yellow) bile, black bile and phlegm. Although this theory has largely been discredited by the medical establishment, the archetype of the Four Humours, linked to the Four Temperaments and the Four Elements, has stood the test of time. The model of the the Four Temperaments (Sanguine, Choleric, Melancholic and Phlegmatic) continues to prove useful in a variety of contexts.

Sanguine (or sanguinous) is linked to blood, to the season of spring (wet and hot) and the element of Air.

Choleric (or bilious) is linked to yellow bile, to the season of summer (dry and hot), and the element of Fire.

Melancholic is linked with black bile, with the season of autumn (dry and cold) and the element of **Earth**.

Phlegmatic is linked with phlegm, with the season of winter (wet and cold), and the element of **Water**.

The Four Temperaments can be very useful in helping us to understand ourselves and each other. It also helps us to appreciate, celebrate and make use of the gifts we have, and those of the people we work with.

However, we should be careful to avoid stereotyping ourselves and those around us. Remember, by nature we are complex and a combination of many things. The Four Temperaments is only one window through which to see people.

An overview of the 4 temperaments

FIRE – The Fire temperament is also thought of as Choleric. People of this temperament are energetic, ambitious and passionate, and often want to instill these values in others. They tend to be doers and as leaders are dynamic and independent, but can be compulsive. They are principled and decisive and want to be right, not popular. Confident and independent, they are not easily discouraged, but can be impatient and quick to anger. At work they tend to be highly goal orientated, with good judgment and decision-making skills. They may be impatient with meetings and other members of staff though, and can be blind to their effect on people around them.

AIR – The Air temperament is also known as Sanguine. Air indicates a personality that is cheerful, talkative and entertaining. Air people are fun-loving and enthusiastic, with good people-skills and a confident and spontaneous flare. They are emotional and demonstrative by nature, but can tend towards arrogance and self-indulgence. At work they provide a positive atmosphere and often volunteer to help out. However they can be day dreamers and battle to complete work, juggling many tasks at once. Their creative and enthusiastic energy can inspire others, but they tend to lose focus on the task when the novelty wears off.

WATER – The Water temperament represents a Phlegmatic personality. People of this temperament are relaxed and easy going. They stay calm and quiet for the most part and can be thought of as all-purpose and able. Although they are slow to anger, if pushed too far they can be explosive. At work they are steady and have a good sense of process and timing. They are good mediators and work well under pressure, but need deadlines to work towards. They sometimes find it hard to be heard in the workplace and will avoid conflict.

EARTH – The Earth temperament is also known as Melancholic. They are deep and thoughtful people who appreciate beauty and are sensitive towards others. They can be philosophical and poetic, self-sacrificing and conscientious. They can become easily depressed and self-critical. They tend to be principled and idealistic. At work they are goal orientated and well organised, with very high standards, keeping their work spaces neat and tidy. They ask difficult questions and are persistent and thorough, being conscious of detail. They can find creative solutions but expect the worst. They may resist change if there is no good precedent.

SOME IDEAS FOR WORKING WITH THE FOUR TEMPERAMENTS MODEL

The model provides workshop participants with a wonderful language for talking about their individual differences and similarities. It has helped many people relax about tense relationships that they experience at work, to appreciate themselves more and to assert themselves more confidently. The model can help to contribute to a more thoughtful and tolerant workplace culture.

The model may also be used when choosing new staff members. It should not be seen as a New Age equivalent of the barrage of psychometric tests that corporate organisations use, but rather as a more gentle set of guidelines as to how people are likely to fit in with the other people that they would be working with.

Chapter 6 has some ideas of how different temperaments respond to change.

A fun Exercise

Try this! Brainstorm all words that you associate with each of the four elements: fire, air, water and earth.... Then ask yourself which of these also describe human qualities. You may come up with words like passionate (fire), cool (water), deep (earth), light (air). Which words more closely describe your qualities?

FOR MORE RESOURCES DON'T FORGET OUR WEBSITE:
www.barefootguide.org

The temperaments chart

FIRE

Emotionally
Dynamic, energetic and active • Very principled • Compulsive need for change • Must correct wrongs • Fears failure • Strong willed and decisive • Not easily discouraged • Independent and self-sufficient • Exudes confidence • Hot, quick to react, impatient • Want to be right, not popular

At Work
Goal oriented, sees the whole picture • Organises well, uses time well • Seeks practical solutions • Moves quickly to action • Delegates work • Makes the goal • Thrives on opposition • Can be blind to their effect on others • Impatient with meetings • Have come with answers • Can create unnecessary work • Good at thinking, judging and deciding

EARTH

Emotionally
Deep and thoughtful • Serious and purposeful • Philosophical and poetic • Appreciative of beauty • Sensitive to others • Self-sacrificing • Easily depressed • Self-critical • Conscientious • Idealistic and principled

At Work
Goal oriented, sees the whole picture • Organises well, uses time well • Schedule and plan orientated • Perfectionist, high standards • Asks the difficult questions • Detail conscious • Persistent and thorough • Orderly and organised • Neat and tidy • Economical • Sees the problems, expects the worst • Finds creative solutions • Likes charts, graphs, figures, lists • Resists change

AIR

Emotionally
Appealing personality • Talkative, storyteller • Life of the party • Good sense of humour • Emotional and demonstrative • Enthusiastic and expressive • Cheerful and bubbling over • Quick to anger but soon forgotten • Curious, changeable

At Work
Provides positive atmosphere • Volunteers for jobs, cannot say no easily • Does many things at once • Struggles to complete work • Gets bored when novelty wears off • Thinks up new activities • Creative and colourful • Energetic and enthusiastic • Inspires others to join • Adaptive but does not know where they stand

WATER

Emotionally
Low-key personality • Easygoing and relaxed • Calm, cool, and collected • Quiet - keeps emotions hidden • All-purpose person • Rhythmic, slow • Slow to anger but explosive when pushed too far

At Work
Steady • good at process, at seeing the whole from beginning to end • Mediates problems • Avoids conflicts • Finds it hard to be heard • Bring good solutions at the right time • Needs deadlines • Good under pressure • Takes time but finds the easy way

PLEASE REMEMBER

- Most people have two dominant temperaments, and one temperament that is much less present. It is the temperaments that are least present that will often help a person find their challenges, e.g. strong water temperaments are often challenged to find their fire, what they really want.

- Temperaments should be used to appreciate the gifts we have and those of others. They can also help us identify our challenges, but should not be used to negatively judge self or others.

- Sometimes your mix of temperaments is hidden by behaviours that were forced on you or adopted as a child, or by sickness or depression. Trying to find your mix of temperaments may take time.

- Functional organisations can really benefit from having a good diversity of temperaments, as they will complement each other in many ways.

WWW.BAREFOOTGUIDE.ORG

The four temperaments at work: tips and challenges

TIPS FOR PEOPLE OF FIERY TEMPERAMENT

- Try to be conscious of your own power and how you affect others emotionally.
- Respect the gifts of other temperaments, especially those that are more careful, less decisive or slow.
- Allow for processes to happen; don't be quick to judge – wait for wider participation.

TIPS FOR WORKING WITH FIERY PEOPLE

- Get straight to the point with them. Be clear and decisive.
- Bring good arguments forward supported by facts and details.
- Don't complain unless absolutely necessary.
- Be prepared to be challenged.
- Think through consequences and back up plans.
- Help them see the need to bring others on board.

TIPS FOR PEOPLE OF AIRY TEMPERAMENT

- Follow through and be complete and comprehensive.
- Find and identify internal and external boundaries.
- Listen deeply and carefully.

TIPS FOR WORKING WITH AIRY PEOPLE

- Be informal and relaxed, don't rush straight to the point.
- Create a positive mood conducive to work.
- Give and facilitate vivid images.
- Don't be too structured.
- Give limits and outlines to change.
- Hold them to deadlines.

TIPS FOR PEOPLE OF EARTHY TEMPERAMENT

- Look beyond the self.
- Look for the lighter side of things.
- Be more self-forgiving

TIPS FOR WORKING WITH EARTHY PEOPLE

- Accept that change will be difficult for them to easily accept.
- Find experiences that link with the new situation.
- Acknowledge and don't begrudge the difficulties of working with the person.
- Give full descriptions of alternative plans you suggest, including their reasons and problems (if there are any).
- Don't be overly positive without reason.
- Use reverse psychology; sometimes feeding resistance and negativity will provoke them to be more positive.

TIPS FOR PEOPLE OF WATERY TEMPERAMENT

- Find your fire!
- Be more action orientated and decisive.
- Pay closer attention to the product.

TIPS FOR WORKING WITH WATERY PEOPLE

- Take your time, don't rush through things.
- Be clear and careful.
- Give important information without too much extraneous detail.
- Give alternatives, as well as time for consideration.
- Don't expect immediate answers, have patience.
- Understand that when the time is right they will move.

THE FOURTH WINDOW

LEADERSHIP POLARITIES

In search of good leadership and facilitation

> *I hear people everywhere saying that the trouble with our time is that there are no great leaders any more. If we look back, we always had them. But to me it seems that there is a very profound reason why there are no great leaders anymore. It is because they are no longer needed. The message is clear. We no longer want to be led from the outside. Each of us must be our own leader. We know enough now to follow the light that's within ourselves, and through this light we will create a new community.*
>
> Lourens van der Post

Lourens van der Post

LOFTY SHARES AN EXPERIENCE OF COLLECTIVE LEADERSHIP

Are leaders and leadership the same thing? Not necessarily. There are so many kinds of leadership.

At CDRA we have monthly reflection sessions where we share our experiences with each other and think about what they mean for our future practice. We often make concrete changes or improvements to our work or organisation on the basis of issues raised at these meetings. This is a form of leadership in which we are all leaders. To me, this seems to be the essence of participatory democracy, where, instead of electing strong leaders, we can create leadership between us.

The challenge is how to ensure that these leadership processes are well designed and facilitated, that they enable all voices to speak, and that they have direction. Perhaps this leads us to a different role for leaders, a different way to bring leadership – a facilitative form of leadership.

The question of leadership seems to be on everyone's lips these days. With our planet in a mess, we need good leadership like never before. But do we need the strongest, toughest leaders, or should we be looking for something else? Strong-arm tactics don't seem to have helped the world lately.

Instead of electing strong leaders, we can create leadership between us.

Understanding the leadership polarities model

A polarity is a relationship between two things that are opposite but not opposing, like night and day, sweet and sour, masculine and feminine, or the fire and water temperaments. Their differences may be interesting but how they co-exist with their differences is more interesting. They are complementary opposites.

In the context of leadership and facilitation, an awareness of leadership polarities can enhance the effectiveness of organisational development work.

The six basic leadership roles, according to the Leadership Polarities model, are:

Inspiring ⟷ Energising
Focusing ⟷ Grounding
Challenging ⟷ Supporting

Holding together opposites and respecting tensions is essential for creative leadership.

These roles relate together according to three sets of polarities: Inspiring/Energising; Focusing/Grounding; Supporting/Challenging.

The diagram over the page provides a simplified model of polarities, demonstrating how the roles and qualities of leadership need to be balanced against each other.

RECOGNISING LEADERSHIP ROLES

INSPIRING — FOCUSING — CHALLENGING

ENERGISING — GROUNDING — SUPPORTING

CHAPTER TWO: INSIDE OUT

Facilitative leadership polarities - roles and qualities

Focusing
(future oriented)

Helping people to plan, to find direction and clarity, to think and strategise about how to get to the future they want, to prioritise

Qualities – concentration, thinking, analysing – earth and fire temperament

Inspiring
(future oriented)

Helping people, (communities, organisations) to find inspiring visions or images of the future to guide their work or lives, to find meaning in their work or lives, hope in themselves.

Qualities – imagination, creativity, story-telling (future stories) – fire and air temperament

Challenging
(future oriented)

Speaking up, positively confronting what is not working, telling the truth, breaking boundaries, asking tough questions, taking risks

Qualities – courage, respect, positivity, questioning – fire, earth and air temperament

Supporting
(present oriented)

Nurturing, empathising, giving comfort, bringing security and safe spaces.

Qualities – empathy, kindness, listening – water and air temperament

Energising
(present oriented)

Helping people to find energy and motivation in what they are doing now. Helping them to remove those things like sexism and racism, oppressive leadership, or poor working conditions that de-energise

Qualities – openness, lack of prejudice, ability to create rhythm – air and water temperament

Grounding
(past oriented)

Helping people, to learn from their experience, to value their history, to accept their mistakes and to forgive and be more thoughtful, so that they may more freely learn.

Qualities – reflection, calming down, objectivity, forgiveness – water and earth temperament

The 6 roles of Facilitative Leadership

INSPIRING - FUTURE ORIENTATION
Helping people, (communities, organisations) to find inspiring visions or images of the future to guide their work or lives, to find meaning in their work or lives, hope in themselves.

VS

ENERGISING - PRESENT ORIENTATION
Helping people to find energy and motivation in what they are doing now. Helping them to remove those things like sexism, racism, oppressive leadership, or poor working conditions that de-energise them.

WHAT WE HAVE LEARNT ABOUT THESE TWO ROLES AND THEIR POLARITY.

Some leaders are good at inspiring (or bringing out inspiration) but get confused when their members or staff seem to lack energy. So members might be excited by the vision of the community or organisation but they could be de-energised by discrimination of some kind. When organisations lack rhythms (like regular staff meetings), they can become erratic, leaving people uncertain, stressed and tired. People get energy from having certain rhythms in their lives.

There can be a healthy tension between these two roles. In a way the energising role is saying to the inspiring role "Great to have you on board but please stay real!" The inspiring role may reply "Ok that's fine but let's not get stuck in the present, the future calls on us to think bigger than we are today!"

FOCUSING - FUTURE ORIENTED
Helping people to plan, to find direction and clarity, to think and strategise about how to get to the future they want, to prioritise.

VS

GROUNDING - PAST ORIENTED
Helping people, to learn from their experience, to value their history, to accept their mistakes and to forgive and be more thoughtful, so that they may more freely learn.

WHAT WE HAVE LEARNT ABOUT THESE TWO ROLES AND THEIR POLARITY.

The relationship between focusing and grounding is closely related to the action-learning cycle (see Chapter 5). A continuous flow of learning from the past into thinking about the future enables a healthy, independent and adaptable organisation or community.

The relationship between these two is cyclical (like night and day). Each must get its required attention for the other to be healthy.

CHALLENGING - FUTURE ORIENTED
Speaking up, positively confronting what is not working, telling the truth, breaking boundaries, asking tough questions, taking risks.

VS

SUPPORTING - PRESENT ORIENTED
Nurturing, empathising, giving comfort, bringing security and safe spaces.

WHAT WE HAVE LEARNT ABOUT THESE TWO ROLES AND THEIR POLARITY.

You should recognise this one immediately. When someone has made a mistake… do they need to be challenged or do they need a supportive arm around them… or do they need a bit of both? If an organisation, leadership or facilitator is too challenging it might feel alienating or too bossy. On the other hand if things are too supportive it might be too comfortable, too sweet or too lenient.

The relationship between these two roles is of complementary opposites. How can we bring sufficient challenge in a positive way to someone but within a supportive environment, so that people do take risks, but are willing to accept honest feedback, knowing that if they fail that they will be supported and not abandoned?

Working with leadership polarities

4 GUIDING THOUGHTS ABOUT INDIVIDUALS

1. EVERYONE IS DIFFERENT.
There is so much diversity in the world. The better we appreciate this diversity the more likely we are to be able to work creatively with it. Diversity is key to healthy organisations.

2. EVERYONE IS INTERESTING.
Scratch below the surface and even apparently dull people have an enlightening story to tell. Finding people boring says more about us than about them.

3. EVERYONE IS EQUALLY WORTHWHILE.
Each person matters (even you!). If you don't believe this you are in the wrong line of work.

4. EVERYONE HAS THE WILL AND ABILITY TO CHANGE AND DEVELOP THEMSELVES.
This may be buried and forgotten – our work is to bring it to the surface.

FOR MORE RESOURCES DON'T FORGET OUR WEBSITE:
www.barefootguide.org

The Leadership Polarities model provides a great source of questions that individuals and organisations can use to assess themselves, celebrate their strengths and work on their challenges.

USING THE MODEL AT THE INDIVIDUAL LEVEL

The organisation (or team) might find the model useful for getting feedback from individuals in the organisation. Encourage people to ask these questions regularly and give feedback to each other.

Inspiring/Energising questions: How inspiring is my work? Do I also have energy day-to-day? Am I doing what I really want to do? What is getting in the way?

Focusing/Grounding questions: Am I focused? Do I have clear direction? Do I know what my priorities are? Am I learning continuously, finding the time to reflect and really learn from experience?

Challenging/Supporting questions: Do I get challenged by others when I need it? Do I allow others to challenge me? Do I ask for or get the support I need?

USING THE MODEL AT AN ORGANISATIONAL LEVEL

The questions are similar, but have a collective orientation. It is often useful, before asking the questions collectively, to get feedback from each individual. It is not unusual for individuals in collective processes to be silent when their answers might be challenging to the more powerful members of the group.

Inspiring/Energising questions: Where is the organisation inspired and purposeful? Where are the conditions of work and the culture motivating or demotivating? What is helping or hindering?

Focusing/Grounding questions: Is the organisation clear and focused? Is it learning from experience in a conscious, ongoing and healthy way that is feeding into our thinking about the future? What is helping or hindering it?

Challenging/Supporting questions: Is there challenge or edge in this organisation? Can we be honest with each other in a positive way? Do we support each other when we struggle or fail?

CHAPTER THREE
People to people

Creating and working with relationships in organisations

> *Love is higher than opinion. If people love one another, the most varied opinions can be reconciled*
>
> Rudolph Steiner

HI, I'M RUBES...

Don't skip this chapter! We are going to try to explore the importance of relationships in organisations and social change... We will talk about "power" in relationships and how to build healthy relationships that make a difference.

CHRISSY TELLS THIS STORY...

Early in my 2-year placement as an OD advisor in Nepal with a local NGO it became clear that the frequent shifts in their purpose as an organisation were most likely a result of an ongoing tug-of-war, an underlying power struggle. The past and current presidents had distinctly different views of the future direction for the NGO, and each had their group of supporters. As personal ties strengthened or weakened one side would appear to be "winning", hence the constant shift in direction and inability to move forward with agreed goals. Being recently arrived I was not, as yet, mixed up in the personal dynamics of the NGO. Many junior staff discussed this power struggle with me as they were able to open up to me as an outsider, as they hadn't been able to do with each other, or with their superiors. With that in mind, and given the sensitivities and personal relationships involved, it was essential that I found a way to subtly and indirectly

"They were able to open up to me as an outsider, as they hadn't been able to do with each other."

CHAPTER THREE: PEOPLE TO PEOPLE

47

bring this issue into our discussions about the NGO's future priorities. Therefore, I slowed down and spent several months simply observing and building relationships in order for people to know me, feel comfortable with me, and trust my motives. It was extremely important to establish a sense of trust between myself and the Board of Directors, which took many months and involved much tea-drinking, suppers in each other's homes and chatting about our families and life in general. Although this initially challenged my Western definition of "productivity" and our usual separation of "work" and "home", I soon realized that this was time very well spent. Connections and friendships between myself and my colleagues developed, adding to our enjoyment of work and appreciation of each other's cultures. And in the long run, such "relationship-building" was a very important part of helping to ensure that the Board would receive my observations about the power struggle described above as constructive and concerned with the NGO's overall health and capacity.

QUESTIONS TO WORK WITH

What really happened here? What was the thinking of the author behind her approach and her actions? What learnings or challenges does this story offer to your practice?

Why are relationships so important?

"Creating and nurturing relationships are also a key purpose of our work and organisation."

Wherever we have warm, trusting and open relationships, all kinds of surprising possibilities begin to open up to us, enabling and unlocking many positive things in ourselves and in others. We find that we can speak more honestly and freely, we can be more of ourselves, more creative, more productive, even more generous. We are less afraid of making mistakes and more able to collectively learn from them.

And of course, when we hide things from each other, where there is a lack of trust, where there is coldness, fear or a lack of clarity, we experience a closing down of possibility and an inability to collectively learn. We feel diminished and less likely to be positive or creative.

Since organisations are a collection of people working together in a purposeful relation it should be obvious that good relationships are vital to healthy organisation and our ability to work together in a purposeful way for achieving our collective, organisational purposes. But are relationships just a means to an end? Think about this.

If the purposes of working together are about building healthy and sustainable community, then *creating and nurturing relationships are also a key purpose of our work and organisation.* In development work, relationships are both means and ends.

HUMAN WARMTH IS THE KEY

In our own experience as leaders and facilitators we have learnt that human warmth is the key to successful development processes. Human warmth enables trust. In situations of change and uncertainty, trust in the one who is facilitating such change is fundamental, whether as a leader or facilitator. Honesty, confidentiality and openness on the part of the leader or facilitator are vital.

More than this, the community or organisation must be surrounded by a cocoon or a womb of warmth in which new beginnings may be gestated, nurtured and given birth. It is for the leader or facilitator to provide or facilitate such warmth, to prove integrity, to generate and encourage more trust, both in the process and more lastingly, in the organisation itself.

The leader or facilitator can model a way of working with people which may be missing within their world. Such warmth begins to allow change to take place beyond the specific actions and techniques of the practitioner. It breaks barriers, dissolves rigidity, and enables people to regain a sense of their own worth.

Relationships of warmth, integrity and trust remind people of their essential humanity and open them to each other and therefore to possible change.

"Human warmth enables trust."

"I observed that by feeling more connected and appreciative of each other, the staff were able to give so much more of themselves."

RUBES TELLS THIS STORY...

A few years ago, when I managed a small team of education support practitioners, I decided that at least once every school term I would organise for all of us to go somewhere for a meal together, to have fun together just as human beings.. Everyone was invited, including the admin and cleaning staff attached to my unit. In no time at all, this became a very popular event. I observed that by feeling more connected and appreciative of each other, the staff were able to give so much more of themselves, while facing the sometimes insurmountable challenges that come with working in a poverty stricken township school district.

Seeing through relationship

Some things are not immediately visible and even the best assessment tools and checklists will not necessarily reveal them.

Relationship is the gateway through which we can begin to see the organisation or community we are working with. By "seeing the organisation" we mean looking through what one would normally see on the surface, like the physical space such as structures, procedures, systems, resources, policies etc., to perceiving the culture and the values, the hidden thinking and assumptions which guide and drive the way the organisation actually thinks and works. These things are not immediately visible and even the best assessment tools and checklists will not reveal them. It is only through getting to know each other on a human level that people will reveal these "secrets" to others.

Simply put, if people trust you they are more likely to say what is really going on.

RUBES TELLS ANOTHER ONE...

I remember an incident which happened to me as a young student teacher on day one of my first practice teaching assignment at a high school in Cape Town. After an initial orientation meeting with the principal, I proceeded to the staff room. It was shortly before the bell would ring for the first interval of the day. The room was empty. Without thinking much I sat on a comfortable couch situated on the window side of the room. The staff room was soon abuzz filling up with teachers, but at the same time I also started to feel a growing sense of unease. Someone sat next to me but barely greeted me, another gave me a cold stare. It soon occurred to me that I might be sitting on the favourite spot of one of the more senior teachers at the school. So I promptly got up, apologised and found a hard chair in a more remote part of the room.

I had done some research on the school before my arrival. I had listened very attentively to the principal during the orientation meeting, but this important "rule" had not been communicated. It was not in any rule book, or prospectus and no checklist would have revealed its existence.

"It hadn't occurred to me that I might be sitting in someone's favourite chair."

Power, relationships and change

If development does not lead to a change in the nature and quality of relationships between people, then it is unlikely that any real development has taken place. If as leaders or facilitators we are not interested in working with relationships, with all their difficulties and complexities, then we risk becoming mere technicians.

This is especially true because power lives in relationship. More often than not development is hampered or stuck because of those power relationships which prevent cooperation, which oppress, stress and limit the potential of people. *Therefore if we want to see shifts or transformation of power we have to help to transform relationships.*

There is no one ideal relationship of power. Different situations demand different kinds of power (see below) and as things change so too should relationships and power change, to meet the new situation.

"If development does not lead to a change in the nature and quality of relationships between people, then it is unlikely that any real development has taken place."

CHAPTER THREE: PEOPLE TO PEOPLE

Dependent, independent and interdependent relationships of power

The three broad phases of individual development described in Chapter Two were characterised as *dependent*, *independent* and *interdependent*. These also describe different relationships of power of people to each other in different phases of life.

When I am *dependent* on you (e.g. for your leadership) then you have power over me (which could be a helpful thing or not). At some point I may start to want to move beyond this dependence, perhaps to develop and express my own leadership, to become more *independent*. When I become more independent it signifies that I have found more power within myself to stand alone. Over time, standing on my own two feet, I may gain the confidence and the ability to relate to you in a more *interdependent* way where power becomes more mutual or shared.

Keeping this in mind can be very helpful for a leader or facilitator. Often in the early phase of a relationship the people or organisations we are working with can feel dependent on us, for guidance, support, access to resources, etc. If our purpose is to be empowering we will want to help people, over time, to become more independent of us, more self-supporting and self-reliant. Quite often we will know this is happening when they start to challenge or criticise us!

This may mean that we have to pull back, giving people space to work with their newly emerging power, to make their own mistakes and learn from them. Should we challenge them to test and strengthen their power? Should we help them to learn when they make mistakes or should we let them find their own way? There are no easy answers to these questions, because it depends on the situation, each requiring a different judgement. But asking these questions is good.

> "Quite often we know that people are becoming empowered when they start to challenge or criticise us!"

THE PERILS OF EMPOWERMENT

Panel 1: WE ARE NOW SUFFICIENTLY EMPOWERED TO BE ABLE TO LET YOU KNOW WHAT A JERK YOU ARE. — YES — A REAL JERK! — PATHETIC — UNINSPIRING — A PAIN IN THE ASS! — AND BOSSY TOO!

Panel 2: ER - THANK YOU FOR SHARING YOUR THOUGHTS WITH ME...

Panel 3: HOW AM I GOING TO RELATE TO THEM NOW? — GULP

IS DEPENDENCE A BAD THING?

Is dependence a bad thing? Well, yes and no. Young children are very dependent on their parents. This phase of dependence can be a wonderful process of learning and teaching, but at some stage, children start to grow up and move towards adulthood and in the process feel the need to move beyond dependence, perhaps before the parent realises it. This movement is often something of a power struggle which, as it becomes resolved, helps children to mature, to strengthen themselves towards adulthood. Keeping children dependent, through overly-mothering and not allowing them to exhibit independent behaviours as they grow up, is not healthy.

Followers are dependent on leaders in all sorts of direct and subtle ways. This may be perfectly healthy until the time comes when they wish and are ready to take more leadership responsibility and power, to shift their relationships to others. Again this often happens with a power struggle, even a crisis, which, if handled well, can also be a healthy process, a testing time to see if people really are ready to take on new roles. Organisations moving from one phase of development to another usually go through these relationship struggles e.g. from dependence on the founder/pioneer to more independent and distributed leadership. This is covered in more depth in Chapter 4.

A word on Victim Power

People who perceive themselves to be unfairly disempowered or marginalised often resort to "victim power". Common examples are: the sulky teenager who mopes around trying to get his parents to feel guilty about some limits they have imposed; or poor communities who overstate their poverty and helplessness in order to extract more resources from outsiders; or employees who continually complain about how stressed and tired they are to get attention and sympathy or to deflect criticism of their work. In each case the "victim" uses indirect or hidden power to stimulate guilt or fear in order to influence the situation in their favour. Their cause may or may not be justified but because it is covert, and easy to deny if confronted, it requires skilful responses by those on the receiving end. People who use victim power are themselves often unaware of other available ways to deal with their situation, in other words, of other powers they may possess.

"... this often happens with a power struggle, even a crisis, which, if handled well, can also be a healthy process, a testing time to see if people really are ready to take on new roles."

QUESTIONS TO WORK WITH
- Where in our lives have we experienced healthy and unhealthy dependent relationships?
- How have we responded to them?
- Do we struggle to talk about power? Why? What can we do to open conversations about power?
- What personal or organisational challenges do we have in seeing and working with power in a helpful way?

FOR MORE RESOURCES DON'T FORGET OUR WEBSITE: www.barefootguide.org

Types of power

There are many ways of seeing power. This is a popular model and connects well with the phases of individual development. In each case the type of power is held in relationship, either over or with others, or with oneself.

POWER OVER

POWER WITHIN

POWER WITH

POWER OVER (dependent power)

Using or exercising one's influence over something or someone. This is how most people see power, and why they don't want to talk about it. But a sculptor exercises power over her medium. The guitarist demonstrates power over his instrument. A mechanic exhibits power over an engine. These are examples of using power over inanimate objects, all positive. Many people use their influence over others for the greater good: Nelson Mandela, Gandhi, Martin Luther King Jr., and Mother Theresa, to name a few.

It is when people abuse power over other people that we see power in a negative light. Power over is not, by definition, bad. Power over only becomes destructive if one is using power irresponsibly, depriving others of meeting their basic needs.

In its destructive form power over is taken as exclusive, conflictual and competitive where the way of getting it is to grab it from someone else or to prevent someone else from exercising their power. Here, power over perpetuates inequality, injustice and poverty. Most often this form of power is exercised when people win exclusive power, when they take power. We even see this happening when people from marginalized communities take power in some way, sometimes adopting the same powerful behaviours as those from whom they have taken power.

POWER WITHIN (independent power)

This kind of power is obtained when developing the inner knowledge, skills and confidence that increase the quality of our lives. Gaining power within includes learning, achieving success, and enjoying the feeling of self-worth that comes with personal growth. Something innate in human beings drives us to set goals, to achieve them, to improve upon what others have done before us, and creatively adapt to new situations – the need for power within. In Chapter One we spoke about development as "as a natural process, an inner power, that we need to read, respect and work with."

POWER WITH (interdependent power)

Achieved when working cooperatively with others. This is also the power of human solidarity, of collective struggles for human rights, and creative collaborations. It is the place where the need for power and the need for love and belonging intersect. If you think of the great achievements of the human race, they all resulted from humans working together or building on the achievements of those who came before them. Power with has to do with finding common ground among different interests and building collective strength.

Healthy organisations and collaboration are an expression of this power as are community struggles and social movements, when they use the unity gained from "power with" in order to counter abusive "power over".

Five bases of power

Social psychologists French and Raven, in a now-classic study (1959), developed a schema of five bases of power which reflect the different bases or resources that power holders rely upon in their relationships with others. Often our power is based on different combinations of these.

Positional Power – this is the formal authority people get from their position in an organisation or society, often backed by policy or law. This is one form of *power over*.

Reward Power – this power depends upon the ability of the power wielder to give valued material rewards, such as money, benefits, time off, desired gifts, promotions or increases in pay or responsibility. In the development sector, this power is particularly held by donors and other intermediaries who distribute funding. It is also *power over*. Some donors who dispense funding do so out of a spirit of solidarity and deep humanity and are uneasy with this power, preferring to develop partnerships based on *power with*. There is a tension in here that has not been resolved in the development world, yet is seldom discussed between the givers and receivers of funding.

Personal Power – the power or ability of people to attract others, to build strong interpersonal relationships, to persuade and build loyalty. This is based on the charisma and interpersonal skills of the power holder. This is an example of *power within*, but it can be used as *power over*. Where the world is becoming more democratic, relying less on positional power and more on consensus, this form of power becomes all the more significant, requiring a deeper focus on individual empowerment.

Expert Power – the power people derive from their skills, knowledge and experience and the organisation's need for those skills and expertise. Unlike the others, this type of power is usually highly specific and limited to the particular area in which the expert is trained and qualified. Being well-informed and up-to-date with useful information is part of this power. This is also an example of *power within* but it can be used as power over (positively or negatively) especially where expert skills and knowledge are perceived to be desperately needed.

Coercive Power – this is the application of negative, fear-based influence on others. It might be based on any of the above power or even physical strength to ensure the obedience of those under power. Coercive power tends to be the most obvious but least effective form of power as it builds resentment and resistance. A covert form of coercive power is the power of victims to use guilt to influence situations in their favour.

> **QUESTIONS TO WORK WITH**
> - What kinds of power do I use and rely on in different relationships in my life?
> - What kinds of power do others use over or with me?
> - What kinds of power are used in the relationships that govern the organisation?
> - What kinds of power do we want to use in different situations in the future?

Why is it important for us to talk about power?

SOME PRACTICAL TIPS

Talking about power is difficult and in some cultures almost impossible. We lack the language and the courage to discuss it because we are afraid it will threaten or disturb our relationships. *Power* is often associated with *coercive, power over,* and so we often prefer to ignore it. There are no easy techniques and tools for this. Hopefully the types and bases of power presented above will provide some language for conversation, prompted by the kinds of questions we have suggested. Like any difficult issue it is good to create a safe and friendly environment and to give time to people to speak. Asking people to express their feelings often guides the conversations to issues that matter. Be careful not to encourage people to accuse each other but rather let them describe what they feel and, if possible, the experiences that gave rise to these feelings.

We often work with people who are or feel disempowered and we accompany and support them in their process of empowerment. We have a role in supporting their efforts to access and exercise their rights and power. Having conversations about power, in a way that makes power transparent and conscious, is a good way of helping people to appreciate the power they have and to use it more positively.

As leaders, facilitators, development professionals and donors we have, and are granted, enormous power by people we try to help, often much more than we realise or even want. Usually it is a combination of *expert* or *reward power*. If we and the people we relate to are not aware of our and their power, its possibilities, limits and potential for misuse, it becomes so easy for us to influence and control them in ways we do not wish to, to have destructive *power over*. For example almost all donor field officers have a story of how a casual thought or suggestion to a community or partner organisation gets taken as an order. Indeed as leaders or facilitators we must be aware that even if we don't intend it, we can change things and even undermine others just by our presence.

TRACEY TELLS THIS STORY...

It was my first week in the office. I was determined to manage in a new way, reduce hierarchy and establish trust. I met every member of staff individually and asked them about their job, their history with the organisation and what they expected of a manager.

Lunch was cooked every day in the office by the guards and the cleaner. It was good local Nepali food but rather bland for my palate after years in Thailand. One day the guard warned me that a particular dish was very 'hot'. No problem, I said, I love spicy food. In fact, the spicier the better. A week later at lunch, I noticed one of the staff members gasping for breath. "I can't understand it", he said, "in the last week the food has got hotter and hotter. I can hardly eat it any more!"

This taught me that when you have "positional power" you have to be very careful what you say!

FINDING OUR POWER WITHIN

As facilitators we relate to community leaders who hold and exercise power (of several kinds) and are mandated by others to exercise their power, whether it is *power over* or *power with*. It is important to help them to exercise their power consciously and responsibly to meet collective goals, one of which may be to encourage and support the empowerment of their members.

Individually, we are all people with power at a personal level, our *power within*. These have been formed and influenced by our experiences and learning processes, both positive and negative. Helping people, whether leaders or members or an organisation, to develop and empower themselves personally is a critical aspect of organisational empowerment and development.

What is needed?

As a leader or facilitator, in order to build authentic developmental relationships, these qualities, attitudes and abilities will really make a difference:

Bring honesty, trustworthiness, integrity... and doubt!

Trust is a defining quality of a good relationship. You can build trust through being worthy of trust in all that you do, and undertake to do – honesty, openness and integrity are key. Many organisations or communities have negative experiences of leaders and outsiders and, despite the warmth they might display towards you, they may find it very difficult to trust and open up to you. But if they do not do so you will be working blindly.

Being completely honest about what you can and can't offer may require courage and frankness. Sometimes as a leader or facilitator you just don't know the answer, and seeking guidance from others can be empowering for them. Being transparent about your own self-doubts can encourage a new degree of honesty in others.

Sometimes as a leader or facilitator you just don't know the answer, and seeking guidance from others can be empowering for them.

CHAPTER THREE: PEOPLE TO PEOPLE

"Feeling embarrassed and bewildered she left and wondered about what it would take to win over the hearts of these embittered people."

RUBES TELLS THIS STORY...

The community's need was clear — they wanted a bridge to be built over the river which tended to flood during the rainy season. Children from the village had to cross the river on their way to school and there had been a recent tragedy of a child drowning. Promises had been made before from local government which had caused great anger among the locals. Since then outsiders were treated with an ample dose of suspicion. So what was the fieldworker supposed to do? She really wanted to help, but could not promise the bridge that they so dearly wanted. Trying to explain what her organisation was about did not help either as this was rather rudely dismissed by the belligerent group which had gathered for the meeting. Feeling embarrassed and bewildered she left and wondered about what it would take to win over the hearts of these embittered people.

Sometimes, as "more resourced" outsiders, when we meet with people suffering from deprivation and confusion we create high expectations, in them and in ourselves. Or we feel completely helpless in not being able to offer any worthwhile assistance and in so doing may even reinforce the hopelessness felt by the people. So what do we do? There are no easy answers to these dilemmas. It might be that we cannot be of help and need to withdraw. We don't come with answers, but if we are to be of any use it will be because people come to trust us and through honest conversation and support we help people to find their own way forward.

Make time your friend

Forming and maintaining trusting relationships not only takes time, but takes quality time. Often leaders or facilitators find it difficult to justify this time to donors as it does not immediately produce visible or easily measurable results.

AND LOFTY TELLS THIS ONE...

The fieldworkers of a successful sustainable agriculture NGO in Zimbabwe that I know put aside good time for building relationships and trying to understand what is happening in the rural districts with which they work. They do not hurry, ensuring a very careful, thorough and deliberate process to really let themselves be known, to get to know the people, their resources and resourcefulness and their circumstances — actually to help the communities to know themselves better. Once this is complete and they have gained deep trust and knowledge of the communities then they are ready to begin their work to support change. This first phase of building relationships and understanding each other can take them up to 18 months. But after this things tend to move very quickly, engaging the communities in the right way and in the right place. They told me that in the 2 to 3 years they work with communities they tend to achieve far more than other NGOs (who start "implementing" much sooner) would achieve in 5 years, if at all.

We are not suggesting that, as facilitators, we always need 18 months to develop good relationships. The point here is that we have to find the time it takes to establish and maintain the quality of relationship required. If we do not manage to do this, and to confidently justify it to board members or funders – we will forever undermine our own ability to be effective. Organisations which employ development practitioners must build the reality of the time it takes to develop and maintain relationships into every aspect of their being and their practice.

Curiosity

Individuals, organisations, communities and partnerships are all complex and deeply fascinating... if we choose to see them as such.

To what extent do we have a real and authentic interest, a deep curiosity in getting to know them? The more curious we are the more potential we have to see and reveal what is really happening.

Remember when you were much younger. As a child, one of the reasons why you were able to learn at a much faster rate than any other time in your development, was through your intense and natural curiosity in the world around you. Remember how many questions you asked, sometimes to the annoyance of your parents and teachers. What happened to that vibrant curiosity – where did it go? As we grow older, and through unfortunate conditioning, the curious child within us sometimes falls asleep and needs to be woken up, lest we become ever slower in our learning.

Being appreciatively curious rather than appearing to be prying or nosey is a clear indication of your intention to learn from another person or group. This is good fuel for relationship building.

Curiosity is infectious... our curiosity may enable people to take more interest in themselves!

Self-awareness of leaders and facilitators

At an organisational level, self-awareness enables organisations to relate to others from a centre of strength.

"Whatever happened to the curiosity of childhood?"

CHAPTER THREE: PEOPLE TO PEOPLE

> Self-respect (ie a good relationship with yourself!) is the foundation for strong relationships with others. If you feel good about yourself, it is much easier to see the good in people and treat them with respect.

ANOTHER ANECDOTE FROM RUBES...

I did some work with a small organisation that had recently been changing the way in which they worked in their programmes. Although they were feeling very excited about these new developments in their practice, they were still not able to articulate it in a coherent and confident manner. As a result, sometimes their own and others' expectations of the organisation became confused or doubtful. An in-depth survey and organisational review process helped them to get in touch with this new and emerging sense of purpose through their changing practice. Essentially I was helping the organisation work on its relationship with itself, both at a human level and at a level of clarity, being more in touch with its own ideas. This is identity work. They came out with a better understanding of how this translates into their programme activities, and importantly, how they presented themselves and related to their target groups.

At an individual level, you have your own strengths and weaknesses, your temperaments, your own likes and dislikes, your own thoughts, feelings and what you want... knowing these will enable you, as a leader or facilitator, to enter more fully and fruitfully into relationships.

Perhaps you are having trouble relating to someone in the organisation and this is hampering your work. It might be that unconsciously they remind you of someone else with whom you have unresolved issues (a bullying father, a deceiving ex-friend...). Perhaps your strong (fire) temperament finds their slow (water) temperament behaviours irritating. In either case the first challenge is one of dealing with yourself, your past or your present or your own nature.

Self-respect (ie a good relationship with yourself!) is the foundation for strong relationships with others. If you feel good about yourself, it is much easier to see the good in people and treat them with respect. If you do not, it is common to project this on to others, finding problems in them that you are having with yourself. All the more reason to know yourself and work on your own development!

> SOMETIMES YOU MAKE ME SO MAD!!

> MAYBE IT'S JUST A QUESTION OF TEMPERAMENT?

Language and culture

Relationships can be hindered or broken over the smallest of misunderstandings. The chances of this happening are amplified if we are from a different culture. It helps to find out whether there are different meanings for the same words in different cultures.

Body language is also important and the way in which things are done. Personal space is very different from culture to culture and standing too close or too far away from someone can affect how we are perceived. In some countries you can get straight down to business, but in many strongly traditional cultures, for example, if you don't go through extended greetings people will not be very open to your suggestions.

Active listening

When was the last time you were really listened to? The kind of listening where the other person was not judging or giving advice too quickly and was genuinely interested in what you had to say, without any agenda other than truly wanting to understand and help you.

RUBES HAS ANOTHER ONE FOR US....

I remember at a party, meeting someone I had not seen for a long time. At these sorts of occasions one tends to have mostly light conversations and move around quite a bit. He had just recently been appointed to a new position of greater responsibility and it was quite apparent that he was both excited and daunted by it. The conversation could have gone one of two ways. His job was very interesting to me and one with which I had good experience. I could have easily put myself in the centre of the discussion, dished out good advice and impressed him with my knowledge. But the conversation would have eventually dried up and we both would have moved on. I opted to go the other way. I really paused and listened to him, putting my own excitement, ideas and experience on hold, offering only a question now and then. He kept on talking, and I somehow became more excited about my listening. Despite all the party buzz around us, the conversation had somehow deepened quite substantially to the point where he started to raise interesting questions about himself and meaningful insights into the challenge he was facing in dealing with a team member. Then I was able to make a few helpful suggestions which he may or may not have found useful. We parted with a satisfied renewal of our relationship and could look forward to more. I was able to go home, having had not only a good time but also a sense of contributing to the development of another person — simply by listening more attentively.

Really trying (and wanting) to listen can become a deeply rewarding experience and is the quickest way to connect to the humanity in others and ourselves.

"Relationships can be broken over the smallest misunderstanding."

FOR MORE RESOURCES DON'T FORGET OUR WEBSITE:
www.barefootguide.org

CHAPTER THREE: PEOPLE TO PEOPLE

What can get in the way?

...of building healthy and respectful relationships

MEMORY OF OTHER RELATIONSHIPS

How often do you reflect, as an organisation on your experience of relationships with other organisations? Just as a person may be very wary in a new relationship when they were betrayed in their previous relationship, so an organisation that has had a failed relationship with another organisation will be cautious in a new one.

LEAVING PROBLEMS TO FESTER

In a relationship things can go badly wrong, leaving hurt and broken trust in its wake. Perhaps an expectation was not met during the implementation of a project. If left unresolved, this will in turn fuel further misunderstanding and negative feelings, intensifying the attitudes that people have of each other.

BLAMING THE OTHER PARTY FOR A DIFFICULT RELATIONSHIP

Blaming another person or group is common but futile. It creates distance and defensiveness, and does not help the relationship develop. If you are not happy about a relationship, it is more useful to think about what you need to do, or not to do, to make it better. You can change your behaviour much more easily than you can persuade someone else to change theirs.

OVERLY TASK-FOCUSSED

Just focussing on the task or project deliverables while excluding the feelings and needs of others is not helpful. Often our jobs are dictated to by narrow project timeframes and deliverables, which create a climate where a task-focus enjoys greater emphasis. However, if you ignore people's feelings and drive through the task regardless, you will alienate others and you will not get the contribution you could get if there was a greater sensitivity to their needs. People are not machines; if you treat them with respect and understanding, and listen to their feelings, they will want to give more and work better together.

MEMORIES OF PREVIOUS HURTS

FESTERING PROBLEMS THAT WON'T GO AWAY

FUTILE FIGHTING

OBSESSION WITH DELIVERABLES

Some practical tips

MEET PEOPLE AT THE HEADS, HEARTS AND FEET

Bring your whole self to relationships. Express what you think, what you feel and what you want and encourage others to do the same, with genuine curiosity and appreciation for what they say.

MEET PEOPLE INFORMALLY

Most people feel relaxed in informal settings. If you have a real interest in developing your relationship then arrange to meet your partner/s in an environment where they are feel comfortable and at home. When people are relaxed they are more able to speak about what is important to them and to be themselves.

IN GROUPS SETTINGS, ENCOURAGE INTEREST IN THE PERSONAL

One of the practices that can be used to facilitate a more open and relaxed environment for working in a group is to ask participants to introduce themselves, and to include what they have left behind at home, office or the field in order to attend the meeting or workshop. This opens up the possibility of sharing some of the feelings that they have. It is not unusual for some to talk about significant issues that are affecting them at that moment, as well as the feelings that go with them. People often also feel relieved when they have been given an opportunity to open up in this way. They feel acknowledged and are better able to put aside some of the frustrations or stresses that might be pulling them away from the work in the group. The group can also feel humanised as they witness a caring environment emerging and as a result the conditions for a good process are established.

IMAGE EXCHANGE

This is a useful technique to use to deal with perceptions and misunderstanding that emerge in a partnership between two organisations.

Write on a flipchart 'How we see ourselves', 'How we see the other group' and 'How we think the other group sees us'. Ask each group to go off and answer these using images and metaphors.

Then meet together in a larger session, show what has been developed and discuss what lies behind it, clearing up misperceptions and tackling problem areas.

BUILDING AGREEMENT

On the left side of a sheet of paper, write down a list of 'things I can do to help you'. Then on the right-hand side, write a list of 'things you could do to help me'. Invite the other person or group to also add to both lists. Then discuss the results and work on the changes.

"I had to remind myself that people are not their behaviours, that they are often caught in relationships or situations that bring out the worst in them."

ONE LAST STORY...

Over the years I have worked with several organisations whose leaders or members shock me by their behaviour, for example being abusive to others or tolerating practices that go against my own value systems. If I did not stop myself I could very easily develop an intense dislike for some of the people I have worked with. But to do so would prevent me from working with them. So in each case I had to choose a different approach. I had to remind myself that people are not their behaviours, that they are often caught in relationships or situations that bring out the worst in them.

Often they fear losing control, not because they are power mad, but because they feel overly responsible and have distrustful relationships. When they act out of fear then they invariably become abusive in some way. So I decide to befriend them, to appreciate whatever it is that they are trying to do right (there is always something). I try to show them trust and in so doing remind them of the benefit of being trusting and trusted. In this position I can give them feedback to help them to see themselves, to understand how they undermine themselves through their behaviours and to discuss alternative ways of relating to others.

CHAPTER FOUR
Through the Looking Glass

Observing and understanding organisations

" *Understanding human needs is half the job of meeting them* "

Adlai Stevenson

HI THERE! I'M KIKI...

This chapter is an eye-opener, really! Full of different "windows", stories, and practical guidelines for helping us understand our organisations, how they grow and develop, and where we can assist if they need to change.

LOFTY TELLS THIS STORY...

My very first contract, as a young freelance organisational development facilitator, began with a phone call from the Director of a local Cape Town NGO. He called me in and told me he was experiencing difficulties with his Admin Team. In his eyes they were underperforming and he wanted me to interview them, find out what the problems were and write a report with recommendations to help "build their capacity."

So I started by interviewing everyone to find the problems. After a while a pattern started to emerge. It seemed to me that the problem lay much more with the Director and his relationships with staff, and very little, as he had supposed, with the staff themselves. He was erratic and sometimes abusive. He sometimes shouted at them and one even burst into tears at the memory. None knew what was really expected of them and they were too afraid to ask. I could see that they felt on edge and undermined, leading to low confidence, silly mistakes, petty resistance and high turnover. I spoke to some of the field-staff and much of what they had said was confirmed.

"It seemed that the problem lay with the Director!"

"Seems this guy is not only disorganised and erratic – he can also be quite abusive. One of their main complaints is that he shouts at them and puts them down in front of other staff members."

After the interviews, which included a general skills audit and a review of the admin systems, I wrote up a report. I described the admin systems as straightforward and workable, and that the skills required to operate them were well within the capabilities of the staff. Then I turned my sights on the Director and his relationships with the staff, boldly exposing what I had been told, with a clever analysis and a synopsis of the interviews (no names mentioned to respect confidentiality), ending with a set of smart recommendations. And all nicely laid out and printed from my new computer system. The report was delivered on time, the next day and I left feeling quite proud of my first job. I expected to be called back to help them implement some of my recommendations.

A day or two later I was tersely summonsed to a meeting by the Director. I arrived, feeling quite nervous, since I had not been thanked for the report yet. I found the Director and the Admin team sitting on one side of a long table and a chair for me on the other. The Director was judge, jury and prosecutor! He was furious with the report and refused to believe the things the staff had said – which they dutifully denied saying under his glare – and then he rejected my analysis and dismissed me. I had been summoned, found guilty and banished!

Looking back I realized that I deserved this treatment – and I am surprised now that they even paid me!

The facilitator turned out to be just as misguided as the Director!

QUESTIONS TO WORK WITH
- What attitudes and values guided the OD facilitator?
- What assumptions did he make about how people change?
- What would you have done differently?
- What were the Director's challenges here in contracting and working with the facilitator?
- What learnings can you draw from this that might be apply to your practice?

LEARNING FROM THIS STORY

Let's unpack this story to see what exactly it was that went wrong.

First, it's clear that the facilitator's methodology, though conventional, was inadequate. First he interviewed the staff and observed their work and organisational systems. Nothing wrong there. Then he analysed the situation and came to some conclusions, based on his own "expert opinion". A common enough thing to do, but this was where the trouble began. The cleverly phrased recommendations and the authoritative tone he adopted in the report made matters worse, because they showed up the Director in a bad light. As a result of the report, which would become a public document within the organisation, the Director was in a tight spot. He was faced with the prospect of a humiliating bring-down in front of his staff. It's hardly surprising that he struck back with the classic "attack is the best form of defence" response.

The facilitator was so intent on exposing the truth and speaking up for the oppressed administrative staff that he didn't take the Director's possible reaction into account. He naively assumed that the truth would set everybody free. Instead, his intervention ended up reinforcing the divide between the Director and the staff, and the organisation was left worse off than before.

WHAT COULD THE FACILITATOR HAVE DONE DIFFERENTLY?

Almost everything. Given that the real issues lay at the deeper level of attitudes, behaviours and relationships, he would have done far better to invest more time in building relationships and developing trust, before he began to formulate his responses. He certainly should have explored those things about the organisation that were working well, and tried to bring to the surface positive stuff that everybody could agree on.

Most important, though, was his relationship with the Director, who, as it turned out, was the person in the organisation who was most in need of help. If the facilitator had gone to speak to him privately and revealed the hard-to-hear things that the staff had said behind closed doors, he might have reacted differently. Given the opportunity to surface his own feelings and experiences, the Director might have been prepared to experiment with a new way of thinking.

"The Director was in a tight spot. He was faced with the prospect of a humiliating bring-down in front of his staff."

CHAPTER FOUR: THROUGH THE LOOKING GLASS

"Was a written report really necessary?"

He might even have ended up apologising to the staff for his rude, authoritarian and inconsiderate behaviour towards them. And, best of all, it might have been revealed that the problems weren't all his fault after all, but the result of a stuck dynamic that brought out the worst in them all.

Had there been a spirit of self-analysis and truth-telling, who knows what might have come out. It could have been a cathartic moment in which they became better able to understand what had happened to their organisation, leading to learning and reconciliation. The staff could then have been invited to make suggestions about how things might be done in future. Concluding his intervention by checking to see if there were still any lingering doubts, fears or resentments, the facilitator could have asked each staff member to say how they felt, before the group moved on to imagining a healthier future, followed by some practical steps to make it happen. To wrap up, there could have been a review to draw learnings from the process, followed by a closing round to allow the staff to rededicate themselves to making the changes work.

WRITTEN REPORTS... DO THEY ALWAYS HELP?

And then there's the matter of the damning report. Was a written report really necessary? Written reports generally help to record resolutions, agreements and proposed steps forward, to note some of the learnings generated by the process. But where there is conflict, a report can serve to entrench polarised attitudes.

Organisations should rather be encouraged to document their own processes and write their own reports. In this way, they can become authors of their own future. Sometimes, an informal written reflection on what happened, what questions surfaced, and maybe even a few tips to help take the learnings forward, can be far more useful than a formal written report.

Sometimes, the best thing is for organisations to document their own processes, write their own reports, and become authors of their own future.

AUTHORS OF OUR OWN FUTURE...

REPORT: "OUR OWN FUTURE"

Facilitating organisational understanding

Some Principles and Guidelines

REVEAL Help the people to better understand themselves and their own organisation, to reveal and share with each other what is really happening.

EXPLORE Help people to explore and understand not only the problems but also to appreciate what is working, as well as future possibilities. This builds hope and confidence when problems have to be faced.

DESCRIBE Help people to take the time to describe what they feel and what behaviours they have observed in themselves, without judging or assessing themselves. Thoughtful observation will allow a rich picture to emerge in a more authentic and less threatening way.

HEAR Make sure that all voices are heard – often the quietest people have the most important information.

SURFACE Help them to surface the history of the organisation, its own story of creation and development. This will help them to collectively learn important lessons and to appreciate their progress rather than measuring themselves against some external standard ("Are we good enough compared to others?"), which can be disheartening and destructive.

BEWARE Beware of simple explanations. Difficult problems often have many or complex causes, some in the past and some in the present, some in reinforcing cycles, or "vicious circles". Many problems we experience are the surface symptoms of deeper problems.

PAY ATTENTION Pay attention to people's feelings – these are the most important clues to lead you to the issues that matter.

Go to www.barefootguide.org Chapter 4 for readings and resources on "Appreciative Inquiry" and "Asset-Based Community Development".

Alternatives to the problem-based approach

Two well-known approaches to change, "Appreciative Inquiry" and "Asset-Based Community Development", in contrast to problem-based approaches, advocate for basing change on what resources exist, what is healthy and living. These can be very fruitful and we support their use. But if used superficially, these approaches can lead to underlying problems being swept under the carpet and an unbalanced and rosy picture emerging. As we will see in Chapter 5 some deeper problematic attitudes, values or assumptions may have to be squarely surfaced, faced, even unlearnt, clearing the way for new change.

Does organisational assessment help anyone?

It has become common for Northern NGOs or donors, who support the development of Southern CBO/NGO partners, to conduct "Organisational Self-Assessments" with their partners. Many frameworks used to analyse or diagnose organisations have been converted into convenient tools and checklists for assessing organisational functioning so that plans could be implemented for improvement to happen.

MOVING BEYOND LIFELESS, TECHNICAL EXERCISES

But these assessments for organisational improvement can digress into lifeless, technical exercises that do not capture the true nature of the organisation. The tools and checklists usually focus more on the formal, visible aspects of an organisation such as its structures, procedures and management systems, especially the financial accounting systems, with the aim of assessing its capacity to manage the funding it gets from the Northern donor. These are the mostly visible aspects of the organisation, but there is also a lot about an organisation that one cannot easily see using such assessment tools, things that are far more influential in determining an organisation's function.

TAKING DIVERSITY INTO ACCOUNT

The assessments tend to measure what the local partner organisation looks like compared to a standard healthy Northern-type professional organisation. But standardised assessments seldom take account of the huge diversity of organisational forms in Southern societies. For instance, the assessment tool might ask whether the organisation has a functioning and registered Board, whereas a more appropriate question might be whether the organisation actually needs a Board in the first place. Perhaps a particular local organisation, being very traditional, is best governed in traditional ways. Or, alternatively, perhaps it is so innovative that it has surpassed the normal conventions and requires a completely different approach.

APPROACHING SOCIAL MOVEMENTS

CBOs and social movements need to be approached with particular care. Often they function best in apparently messy and disorganised ways when compared with "efficient" professional organisations. As such they enable ordinary non-professional people to lead and participate. Imported assessments can steer such organisations into becoming ineffective professional clones, losing their local ways and their connection with the people.

MATTERS OF JUDGEMENT

Assessment is judgemental and since organisations are never perfect, there will always be gaps in every aspect. As a result of assessments organisations are often left feeling inadequate and undermined. Besides, the measures used are almost always imported and seldom developed by

"Often assessment for improvement can digress into a lifeless, technical exercise that does not capture the true nature of the organisation."

the local CBO/NGO, using its own ideas of what is valid and useful. For example, when CDRA assessed its own organisation, which it felt to be fairly healthy, using one of the most common instruments (OCAT), the practitioners were surprised to see that they had scored low marks in areas where they knew themselves to be strong and unique.

Formalised instruments are often unable to take account of progress over time, i.e. the story or biography of the organisation. Why is this important? Well, a CBO/NGO might get low scores from the checklist, and think that they need help in certain areas. But maybe if they had been scored a year earlier it would reveal that they had improved significantly since then in these areas and will continue to improve, if left alone. A "static" assessment can be very destructive, undermining the important gains an organisation has made.

> "Outsiders who bring external assessment instruments, even like the ones in this book, must be careful not to undermine local ways of seeing."

AVOIDING THE SIMPLISTIC DIAGNOSIS

Simplistic diagnosis – for example, "the staff are under-performing in their field-work because they lack skills" – can throw everyone off track. The assessment instrument might lead them to conclude that they need more skills training, whereas their skills may be technically fine and the reasons they are under-performing are deeper, relating to a lack of confidence, being over-worked, or unsure of what is expected of them. Instruments that tend to compartmentalise problems can easily fail to surface deeper causes.

Outsiders who bring external assessment instruments, even like the ones in this book, must be careful not to undermine people's own ways of seeing themselves. At the end of this chapter we describe some approaches which can integrate well with local ways of seeing. Organisations are so much more interesting and complex than these often rather lifeless tools are able to reveal. We need to expand our abilities to fully appreciate organisations as wonderful creations of human nature.

FOR MORE RESOURCES DON'T FORGET OUR WEBSITE:
www.barefootguide.org

CHRISSY RELATES THIS STORY FROM EAST AFRICA

"Whose assessment is this, anyway?"

This story comes from my days as a program officer with a Canadian international development organisation that worked through volunteers, providing accompaniment and training to build staff skills.

Back when my organisation was newly excited about this emerging trend of organisational assessments (OA), we set out to "experiment" by testing an OA survey with one of our long-standing partner organisations in East Africa. This organisation was a small community-based organisation, working in a rural situation with programmes that spread from HIV-AIDS to micro-credit, plus IT training and other vocational training for youth. They were led by a charismatic leader who was very inspiring and dynamic.

My director visited this partner for 2 days and conducted the OA survey with them. Due to the time constraints, there were several 1:1 conversations with long-serving members of the organisation but largely the survey was completed by my director based on her observations. She returned to our office, filled in the survey and assigned the corresponding scores, as directed by this OA tool. Once the results were tallied up, she found that this organisation scored in the "very weak" category and this created serious doubt for her that such a small struggling organisation would be able to "absorb" our capacity building support. Several of the staff had shared with her during the OA that staff were working without consistent salaries, and many were disillusioned and preparing to leave the organisation. Thus, how was our work with them sustainable?

So the partnership was questioned and upcoming activities were cancelled. She instructed me, the program officer responsible for this partnership, to prepare an exit strategy from the partnership. I felt this was an unfair use of the organisational assessment, as we had begun using OA tools as a way to better understanding the strengths and weaknesses of our partner so we could design more appropriate interventions to support them. But instead, we were using this OA as a tool for our own decision-making about partnerships, and in effect, using their weaknesses against them.

I lobbied hard to be able to return to this organisation and spend more time with them, and use other methods of organisational understanding beyond this OA survey. They were understandably wary of this second process, as several important activities had been cancelled after my director's visit. I tried to bring back the spirit of a self-reflective assessment into the process, and also shared examples of my own organisation's strengths and weaknesses, so as to make this more of a mutual exercise of understanding. So we spent time together, conducting interviews with all the staff, holding workshops and coming to a shared understanding of the key issues on the horizon for the organisation. At the end of it, the organisation had developed a shared understanding of their strengths and weaknesses and ended up deciding that they wanted to build linkages with several local capacity building organisations who could offer the specific resources they felt they needed to grow and overcome their challenges. In effect, this signaled a change and an eventual end to our partnership with them, but this was more of a mutual decision than the harsh conclusion reached by my director after the first visit.

Too many of us INGOs neglect to "check our power at the door" when we facilitate organisational assessments. We must work hard to live up to the standards we have set for partnerships and do more than pay lip service to concepts of sovereignty and mutuality.

TWO WINDOWS...

THROUGH WHICH TO READ ORGANISATIONS

In Chapter One we described the organisation as a living system with several characteristics. These included its values and principles, its actual practice, its human relationships, culture and habits, and its stage of development. We also noted that these characteristics lie underneath the more visible aspects such as its structure, its governance and decision-making procedures, and the formal policies and systems and frameworks through which it is planned and organised.

We present here two models for looking at organisations – windows to help us to see these key characteristics more clearly. For those readers who feel that the more visible aspects are getting sidelined in favour of the less visible, be patient. It will become apparent that in understanding the life history, life cycles, culture and relationships of an organisation a whole picture starts to emerge in which the more visible and formal aspects are also revealed, in an even clearer light.

Each Window helps us to ask different questions of the organisations we are working with. Through the first Window we look at the Phases of Development of Organisations, how they develop and change over time – much like the Individual Development Phases Window in Chapter Two. The second Window looks onto the key Elements and Cycles of Organisations, as a way of seeing an organisation at work. This second Window may remind you of the Head, Heart, Feet model. Each Window complements the other to help provide a more comprehensive picture of an organisation in time and space.

PHASES OF DEVELOPMENT OF ORGANISATIONS

KEY ELEMENTS AND CYCLES OF ORGANISATIONS

CHAPTER FOUR: THROUGH THE LOOKING GLASS

THE FIRST WINDOW

THE PHASES OF ORGANISATION DEVELOPMENT
How do organisations grow and develop?

Organisations are like human beings. They are born, grow up and eventually pass away. In Chapter Two we mentioned that individuals go through three general stages of development – the dependent, independent and interdependent stages. In the same way, organisations go through similar stages, or phases.

The acclaimed organisational practitioners, Bernard Lievegoed and Fritz Glasl, through their observations of many organisations, were able to distinguish four general phases of organisational development: The Pioneering Phase, the Rational Phase, the Integrated Phase, and the Associative Phase.

> **THE PHASES IN BRIEF**
> 1. **THE PIONEERING PHASE** This phase is like a flowering patch – messy but fresh with new energy. It's flexible, but dependent on the pioneer, who is seen as a parental figure.
> 2. **THE RATIONAL PHASE** "Left-right-left-right!" Organisations in this phase are independent, more conscious and well organised.
> 3. **THE INTEGRATED PHASE** Like a good stew, this phase is a mix of the best. Organisations in this phase are interdependent, organised but more flexible.
> 4. **THE ASSOCIATIVE PHASE** Organisations in this phase are interdependent and better connected to their environment.
>
> Take a look at the diagram on Pages 80-81 to get an overview of the phases.

Unlike with human beings, organisations do not have to move from one Phase to another. Some, like small CBOs or NGOs, or professional agencies like architects or doctors, may happily stay in the Pioneering Phase, while others, like Government Departments, may do well to stay in the Rational Phase.

Bernard Lievegoed — Fritz Glasl

The Pioneering Phase

THE EARLY YEARS

This is like the first part of a person's life: being born, growing up, becoming a young adult. The first phase of a successful initiative is often vibrant, exciting, full of surprises and growth. The pioneer, usually one person, though sometimes two, starts the venture with motivation, high energy and a big idea of what he or she wants to achieve. Pioneers gather enthusiasts around them, often trusted friends, and invest great time and commitment in the new birth.

The pioneering organisation often has a family atmosphere about it and can be quite informal, without clear policies or procedures. Meetings happen on the spot, depending on the needs of the day. Plans are made on the fly and a great deal of experimentation takes place. Pioneers are expected – and prepared – to make decisions immediately without much discussion. This is a very creative, fast and flexible phase with different people playing different roles at different times.

GROWTH AND CRISIS

If the organisation is successful it attracts resources and often grows at a rapid rate. But with growth, problems arise over time. New people are employed who do not share the initial joys and struggles of the early days. As more people join, the sense of intimacy is lost. The family feeling starts to disappear and very often conflict begins to develop between the old and new generations.

As the workload and staff numbers grow, things become more complex and difficulties arise. But the pioneer may not wish to let go of the informal way of managing – he or she still wants to remain in charge in his or her own way. But new staff, increasingly empowered by their experience, may also want to make some decisions and take over managing the work they are responsible for.

Other problems start to crop up. Things can become chaotic and too disorganised. New levels of planning and organised support are needed to cope with the growth and increasing complexity of the work, including clearly understood goals and policies to enable people to work together. This may be resisted by the pioneer and original staff who fondly remember the early informal days. Motivation decreases and conflicts increase.

LEADERSHIP AND FACILITATION OF THE CRISIS

In Chapter One (page 20) we talked about emergent and transformative change. The Pioneering Phase largely involves an emergent type of change, which typically culminates in a crisis which has the potential for transformative change. In this way, the organisation transforms itself as it enters the Rational Phase.

If the leadership is able to appreciate the crisis and see the need for transformation, the organisation is enabled to move through the crisis, albeit with some pain, into a new phase of growth.

"Insisting that a pioneering organisation becomes more organised sooner than it needs to be, or trying to force it to the next phase, is a bit like parents who push a child to behave like an adult before the time is right."

Sometimes the crisis is sufficiently disruptive that the organisations sees the need to call upon the help of outside an facilitator to guide them through the change process. This can be a good thing, and can prevent a destructive implosion. For the facilitator who is called in to work with the organisation in crisis, the immediate task is to acknowledge and understand all the competing feelings and ideas that are washing around inside the organisation. To enable these to be transformed into the next phase, it is important to see the crisis as a natural part of the organisation's development, rather than a failure.

Here the facilitator should help the organisation to read and understand which of the aspects of the pioneering organisation should be appreciated and kept and which are not working and need to be let go of or "unlearnt". This will clear the way for a new set of organisational principles and values to take root. This process of change, known as the U-process, is dealt with in Chapter 5.

If this crisis is not well navigated, the organisation can die. This can be exacerbated by donors withdrawing their support under the false impression that the organisation is failing. Sometimes, long before a crisis has set in, donors or naive leaders can inadvertently provoke a different kind of crisis by insisting that a pioneering organisation becomes more organised sooner than it needs to, or trying to force it to the Rational Phase. This is a bit like parents who push a child to behave like an adult before the time is right! It can result in the pioneering energy and spirit of the organisation being stifled, and can force a lively organisation into a deadening bureaucratic mode where all enthusiasm is lost.

Sometimes pioneers refuse to change their leadership style and lose their unhappy staff, either leading to collapse or forcing the organisation to restart, repeating the phase.

The Rational Phase

THE EARLY YEARS

If the organisation has weathered the storm of the pioneering crisis and if leadership has accepted the need for change, then it can move more fully into this next phase. Quite often the pioneer leaves during the crisis and goes on to start another organisation (it's what they like to do), making way for a new leader.

This phase is about moving from the personal, intuitive, experimental way of organisation to a more objective, conscious, clear and planned way of meeting the growing organisation's objectives.

In the Rational Phase we start to see shared and written goals and policies, clear decision-making, systems, procedural handbooks, and formal reporting relationships being called for. The vision, identity and purpose of the organisation are made more conscious. Clear leadership functions regarding plans, procedures, goals, policies, organisation, evaluation and review are developed.

Staff have more specialised functions in this phase. Departments and new layers of management are established to divide the work more manageably. New leadership is promoted as it's no longer possible for everything to be initiated, decided and led by the pioneer. This is what is meant by differentiation. New integrative functions, like inter-departmental meetings, have to be held to counter the isolation that comes from this differentiation.

Essentially, in this phase, the organisation gets its act together in a more conscious and planned way. It's not necessarily an easy process, as there may be staff who resist because they feel that the organisation is becoming a bureaucracy. Certainly, the challenge is to avoid becoming machine-like and alienating, so it's important to listen to all points of view to keep the organisation healthy and lively. Older staff may speak with nostalgia about the old family days! Keeping some of the human touches of the Pioneering Phase may be worthwhile to bring balance to this phase.

Rational organisations do not have to be alienating bureaucracies, though they often develop into them, as we shall see below. They can be highly productive, well-organised and healthy establishments.

This phase can lead to great expansion in both size and complexity as the organisation frees up new energy in its more differentiated way of working. Most of the very large organisations in the world today trace their biggest expansions to this phase.

GROWTH AND CRISIS

Over time a new kind of crisis may begin to set in. Through differentiation, the pioneer's ideas are scattered and the other parts of the organisation have to "carry" the impulse consciously. They do this by taking responsibility for implementing an aspect of the whole. But what happens is that they can become stuck in seeing only the aspect that they are responsible for. In this way the collective sense of purpose fragments and the organisation can begin to grow in lopsided ways.

Problems typically arise as the organisation differentiates through increasingly "efficient" mechanistic structures, systems, policies and procedures. Tension starts to develop as staff, who have become more experienced and empowered in the process, become frustrated with the hierarchies of communication and decision-making, and the division of work into competing silos. These silos may have been helpful in tidying up the chaos of the previous phase, but now they become obstructive. People start feeling dissatisfied and disconnected from the purpose of their work and lose touch with the impact of the organisation as a whole, becoming stuck and isolated in the process. Many people can start to feel like lonely or disgruntled cogs in a creaking machine.

Staff may then start to challenge or break the rules. Often the response by management is to crack down, strengthening the rules and trying to enforce compliance. Staff may succumb to this but it is likely to lead to hidden resistance by way of a loss of vitality, decreased motivation and low productivity, higher levels of absenteeism or turnover and increased communication difficulties. A vicious cycle can set in. "Office politics" and corridor gossip become the centre of a shadow organisation. We call this a "cold crisis".

On the other hand the situation may develop into a "hot crisis" of more open challenge and resistance, even conflict, also resulting in a loss of productivity, perhaps even work stoppages and protests.

Either way the crisis deepens and something has to give way.

"Staff may begin to grumble and challenge or break the rules."

> "Many people who instinctively don't like this phase may be tempted, when problems arise, to see this as the end-of-phase crisis and then get themselves ready for the next (sexier looking) Integrated Phase."

LEADERSHIP AND FACILITATION OF THE CRISIS

Many people (in this post-modern age) instinctively don't like this Rational Phase when they experience it or even when it is described to them – it feels mechanistic and old-school. So they may be tempted, when problems arise, to see organisational problems as the end-of-phase crisis and then get themselves ready for the next (sexier looking) Integrated Phase. But these problems may just need fixing. There are healthy forms of this Rational Phase, where organisations maintain human relationships and processes to balance the more mechanistic features of the phase.

But when the staff have reached a level of both empowerment and frustration and the levels of hot or cold crisis are high enough that productivity is falling consistently, it begins to make sense to transform the organisation, to move into the Integrated Phase. This will help break down the divisions and mobilise the more developed capabilities of the staff through a different quality of organisation.

Again it is quite possible that external facilitation is needed to assist the organisation to navigate the phase.

The challenge of leading or facilitating this crisis is similar to the crisis of the previous phase: appreciating and keeping what works and unlearning what does not, clearing the way for the new set of organisational principles and features that characterises the next phase to take root. (Another example of the U-process of change is decribed in Chapter 5.)

Many, if not most, of the leadership and management books available today focus on this crisis as experienced by big business corporates, describing their challenge to move to the Integrated Phase. Unfortunately these books get used by many organisations who are working from the Pioneering to the Rational Phase, so that the advice they get from these books is sometimes the very opposite of what they need!

> "The organisation of the Integrated Phase is held together by strong common vision, purpose and values more than the rules and policies of the Rational Phase."

The Integrated Phase

THE EARLY YEARS

This phase is an integration of the best features of the Pioneering and Rational Phases. It is more human and efficient and therefore more effective in mobilising the diverse capabilities of more mature staff and relationships.

The more empowered staff will tend to want flatter, simpler, decentralised structures that facilitate fluid communication and collaboration.

This may end up looking like a network of pioneering teams or units with a smaller and more facilitative hierarchy. The organisation of the Integrated Phase is held together by a strong common vision, and by a sense of purpose and values, rather than by the rules, procedures and policies of the Rational Phase.

GROWTH AND CRISIS

The crisis of the Integrated Phase comes not from within the organisation but rather because it is isolated from its environment, from other organisations (perhaps as competitors). Here the issues, crises and opportunities for further development come from new forms of cooperation and collaboration with other organisations.

LEADERSHIP AND FACILITATION OF THE CRISIS

An organisation that has reached this phase is likely to be peopled by a diverse range of mature and talented people, possibly quite proud of their achievements and their particular "brand". The challenge is for them to let go of their competitive urges and pride in order to team up with other organisations. This will require a particularly visionary and wise leadership and facilitation.

The Associative Phase

There is a growing realisation of our common and shared destiny in the increasingly globalised world and therefore the need for interdependent relationships that connect different organisations across an ever-widening spectrum, into creative and authentic partnerships. We need to work together in order to achieve the social harmony and sustainable development that will protect us and our planet into the future.

The idea of partnerships and collaborations across organisations has been promoted for a long time and many attempts have been made to make these real, but with great difficulty. Some have begun to succeed but not many of us have reached the mature or full forms of this phase. But there is growing urgency for us to begin to discover the principles, values and forms of these new organisational types.

"There is a growing realisation of our common and shared destiny in the increasingly globalised world and therefore the need for interdependent relationships that connect different organisations across an ever-widening spectrum, into creative and authentic partnerships."

Phases of organisational development

PIONEERING PHASE CRISIS

- The sense of intimacy is lost, conflict develops between old and new generations.
- Growing complexity no longer met by informal way of managing.
- Chaos and disorganisation increase.
- Loss in confidence in pioneer's ability
- New staff, want some decision-making power
- Pioneer and original staff resist change,
- Motivation decreases and conflicts increase.

RATIONAL PHASE CRISIS

- The collective sense of purpose fragments
- Mechanistic structures, systems, policies and procedures begin to frustrate the staff
- People start feeling stuck and isolated in the process, cogs in a creaking machine.
- Staff start to challenge or break the rules. Management cracks down.
- Often hidden resistance, loss of vitality and productivity
- Corridor gossip and "cold crisis" can set in.
- Or a "hot crisis" of more open challenge and resistance.

CRISIS

FEATURES OF THE PIONEERING PHASE

- Small, close to the community / clients
- Personality of pioneer shapes structure, ways of working
- Charismatic leadership
- Highly personalised functions organised around the abilities of staff
- Improvising — flexible - dependent

Challenges: chaos, arbitrariness, dependence of staff

FEATURES OF THE RATIONAL PHASE

- Structures and roles become formalised
- Guided by policies
- Differentiated management, business-like, rational, division of labour
- Staff fit into organisational requirements
- Controlling — systematic - independent

Challenges: over-organisation, fragmentation, bureaucracy

The Pioneering Phase

The Rational Phase

Growth phases and developmental crises

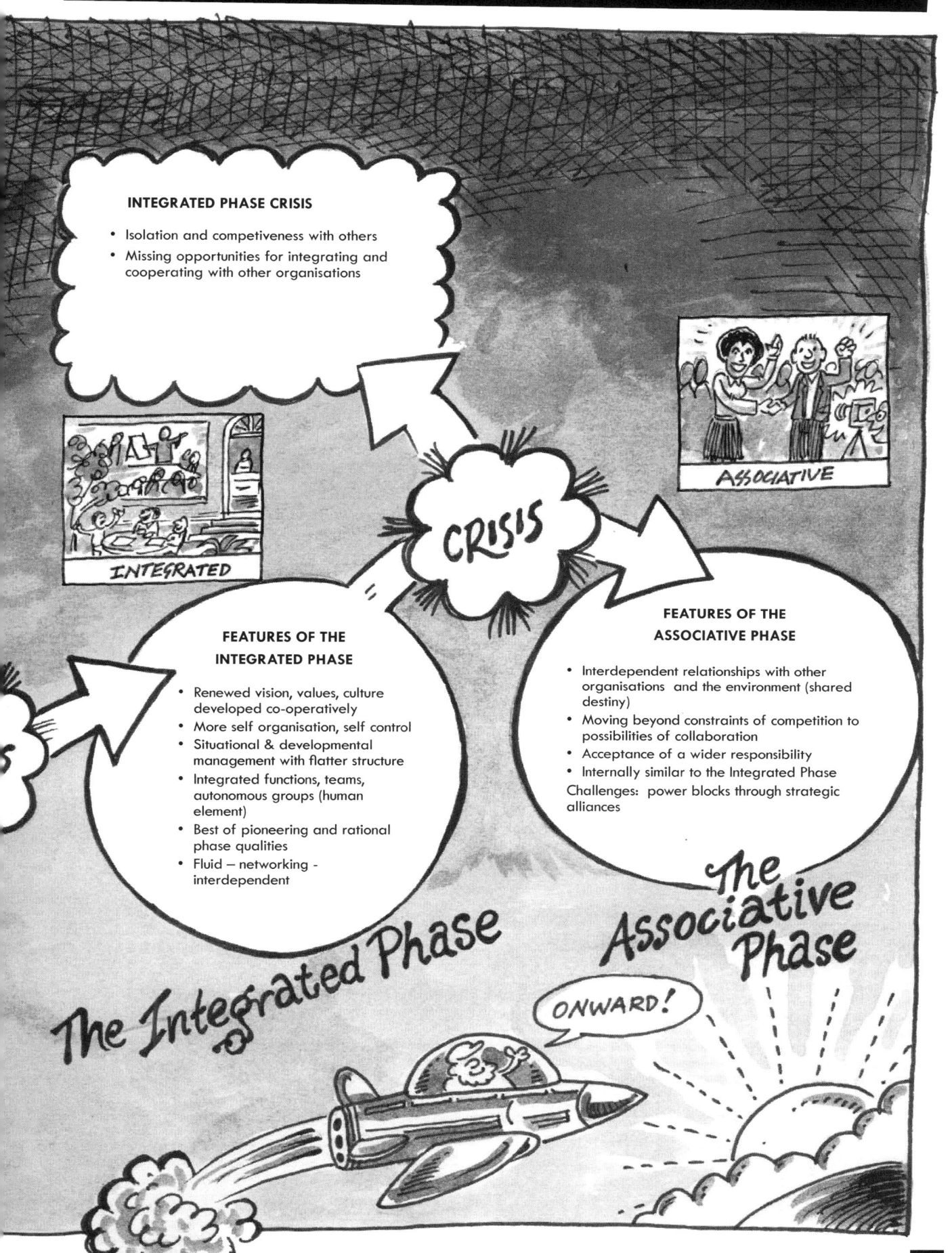

INTEGRATED PHASE CRISIS

- Isolation and competiveness with others
- Missing opportunities for integrating and cooperating with other organisations

INTEGRATED

ASSOCIATIVE

CRISIS

FEATURES OF THE INTEGRATED PHASE

- Renewed vision, values, culture developed co-operatively
- More self organisation, self control
- Situational & developmental management with flatter structure
- Integrated functions, teams, autonomous groups (human element)
- Best of pioneering and rational phase qualities
- Fluid – networking - interdependent

FEATURES OF THE ASSOCIATIVE PHASE

- Interdependent relationships with other organisations and the environment (shared destiny)
- Moving beyond constraints of competition to possibilities of collaboration
- Acceptance of a wider responsibility
- Internally similar to the Integrated Phase

Challenges: power blocks through strategic alliances

The Integrated Phase

The Associative Phase

ONWARD!

Frequently asked questions about the phases

CAN OUR ORGANISATION JUMP FROM THE PIONEERING PHASE TO THE INTEGRATED OR ASSOCIATIVE PHASE?

People frequently ask this question because these later phases sound so cool, so in line with their thinking. The answer is generally "no", but occasionally a "yes" will be appropriate. You can't skip teenagerhood even if, as a child, you may sometimes want to be an adult. In the same way, organisations can't jump a phase, simply because in that phase there are important lessons to be learnt and capabilities to be developed that are required for the next phase. But, if your organisation has employed more experienced people, and if you have invested good time in learning in the Rational Phase, and have tried to introduce more human-centred working conditions, there is no reason why you should not be able to move more quickly and easily to the next phase. Sensible features more often found in the Integrated Phase, like flexible teamworking, can be introduced in the Rational Phase.

Organisations can also be associative with other organisations at any stage in their development, but this will not come easily or naturally until they reach the Associative Phase.

CAN OUR ORGANISATION REMAIN IN THE SAME PHASE?

It may seem natural that all organisations, like individuals, should move through all the phases, but this is not necessarily the case. Most government departments, for instance, should probably remain in the Rational Phase, as this may be the best organisational form to get the task done. Similarly, smaller and more nimble NGOs and community based organisations may happily remain in the Pioneer Phase. Over time they may adopt some or other characteristics of "later" phases, e.g. being more associative, but still remain essentially pioneering.

CAN THE ORGANISATION SKIP OR AVOID A CRISIS?

No, these crises are a natural and unavoidable feature of development. But you can prevent a crisis from destroying an organisation. Crises enable you to unlearn what you have to let go of and they stir up the energy you need to launch yourself into the next phase. A good leader should be able to anticipate such a crisis and (with or without the help of external facilitation) be able to ensure that the crisis does not get mis-read and mishandled into a disaster.

CAN AN ORGANISATION BE IN MORE THAN ONE PHASE AT A TIME?

It is quite common for large organisations to have different parts (departments) at different stages of development. A new section or department may be created to establish a new product or service and the practices and culture of this department may be quite similar to those of organisations in the pioneering phase of development. While this is happening the larger parent organisation may be going through the crisis of the Rational Phase.

WHAT HAPPENS WHEN AN ORGANISATION DIES?

Death is never an easy thing to deal with, but sometimes has to be faced. In our work with organisations in the development sector, we are often faced with stagnation: the refusal of old ideas to die, people hanging on to past glories. We see organisations whose original life forces have dried up but who are kept on life-support by funders, others who are sustained by little more than the memories of long-gone success, or those held together against all odds by ageing leaders who cannot separate their own identities from the withered structures that are all that remain of the major achievements of their lives, and who simply cannot bear the final judgement of closure. If we are called upon to assist with these organisations our work becomes more clerical in nature. Our task is to help the people to find a good death, a gentle death, in effect, to conduct a funeral.

IS THERE SUCH A THING AS THE "GOOD DEATH" OF AN ORGANISATION?

Like a good funeral, the "good death" of an organisation requires an appreciation of what it achieved, and a celebration of its life, as well as an honest assessment from which important learnings can emerge. Like any good funeral there must be a space for people to express their grief and regret and in doing so begin to clear the space for new life. The good death of an organisation should free people from the burden of guilt, regret and blame for any failures. It should be a gentle process of resolving and forgiving, of letting go, bearing in mind that new organisations often spring up from nowhere to take up the space that opens up when the old organisation is finally laid to rest.

"Like any good funeral it must be a space for people to express their grief and regret and in doing so to begin to clear the space for new life."

Using the Phases of Development in Practice

SOME TIPS AND TECHNIQUES

Do not assume that if you have a crisis in the organisation that you need to transform to the next phase! As a leader or facilitator working with crisis the first thing is to see whether what you are facing is perhaps just a normal difficulty that requires some good problem-solving.

If you are sure you are in a crisis of a phase of development then it may be worthwhile to share this framework with members of the organisation and ask them what challenges they think need to be faced. This can help people to see that what they are going through is normal and thus reduce anxiety, helping to prevent people from blaming each other (especially leadership) for all the troubles.

This Phases Window also gives some glimpse into a possible future – it can inspire hope. However, be careful that people do not immediately try to rethink the organisation using these new ideas without a meaningful process of dealing with the crisis – by surfacing the hidden feelings and dynamics and helping people to let go of what is underneath the crisis. If things are rushed then the organisation may easily slip back into the old ways and crisis.

DOING AN ORGANISATIONAL BIOGRAPHY

One of the most powerful exercises to help an organisation to understand its process of development is to do an Organisational Biography. In Chapter 2 we introduced the idea of Biography Work to help us to understand the life-cycle of an individual. We can do the same with organisations. Such a process almost always leaves people feeling more connected and appreciative of how the organisation has developed, the contribution of leaders, surfacing good learnings, and building a deeper understanding of the story behind the situation it finds itself in today.

ORGANISATIONAL BIOGRAPHY:

A USEFUL TOOL

Use it to describe an organisation as a picture over time to gain an insight into the phases in the organisation's development

Use it to examine any turning points or crises in the life of the organisation and to try to understand how these impacted on where the organisation is now and what it can learn from these crises to move into the future

---

Go to www.barefoot.org for "Organisation biography development exercise for OD Fieldguide.doc"

THE SECOND WINDOW

ORGANISATIONAL ELEMENTS AND CYCLES

Every human being is unique, but in many fundamental ways we are all very similar. The same can be said of organisations. This section is a window into the fundamental features of organisations, their underlying form and functioning.

Take a quick look at the Organisational Elements and Cycles diagram on page 91. See if you can figure it out before reading the detail below.

In this section we describe six fundamental elements of organisation. The last of these includes three cycles:

1. Organisational Identity
2. Understanding the Context
3. Purpose
4. Strategy and Approaches
5. Programme Activities, Capacities and Resources
6. Developing and Managing Practice, including 3 cycles
   (i) Planning (strategic and operational),
   (ii) Monitoring,
   (iii) Evaluation.

Each of these elements and cycles is like a pane of glass through which to more closely examine your organisation.

1. Organisational Identity

Sovereign organisations tend to have a strong sense of their own identity, in other words what the organisation collectively thinks, feels and wants, and as a result are able to act on these things. Good leaders are able to facilitate an increasing sense of identity, providing deep bonds between members.

This is the inner core of the organisation, and can be said to exist at three levels:

THE HEAD: Principles and Leading Ideas

These are the organisation's guiding ideas and essential concepts that underpin their thinking. For example: "You cannot deliver development. People are already developing and can only develop themselves", or: "As in nature, the principle of diversity depends on rich diversities of people for its healthy survival".

THE HEART: Values, Culture and Relationships.

An organisation may aspire to live by a set of values that matter to it, like respect for different opinions, transparency and honesty. Often values that are expressed are difficult to put into practice. For example, an

---

Using this Window

This model can be used as a guide for seeing, exploring, understanding an organisation, and for identifying areas of inquiry when change is needed. It can also be used as a reference point for leaders wanting to keep in mind important aspects of organisational life which may slip from view in the daily busyness of work — many of the key characteristics of organisations are not easily visible and are easy to lose sight of.

organisation might value transparency while in practice managers tend to prefer confidentiality. Or an organisation may try to promote cooperation while in practice its staff members act in a competitive way.

Values determine the relationships and culture of an organisation. People often talk about "the unique way we do things around here", but one has to ask: what really matters to the organisation? What beliefs, whether positive or negative, guide the actual behaviour and actions of the organisation? What values are being contested or are in tension? Values are often in polarity with each other, such as transparency and confidentiality, or collective consensus and individual freedom, within the same organisation. Healthy organisations often try to embrace such polarities. A lot can be understood about an organisation by looking at how it deals with these tensions.

As a leader or facilitator it is worth paying particular attention to the lived values, relationships and culture of an organisation, unearthing not just what people say but how they behave and treat each other, as people. If you can help the organisation to get this right, an inner foundation will be laid to support the healthy development of the organisation as a whole.

THE FEET: The Work we Want to Do

What is the work that the people in the organisation really want to do? Too often we find organisations doing what donors pay them to do rather than what the staff or members wish to do. Or someone takes a job or position in the organisation not because they like the work but because it pays the bills or gives them status. While you can't blame people for taking the best job they can get, the organisation will suffer if the staff are not really interested in the organisation's real work.

Most organisations are comprised of a diverse range of people and thus contain within themselves a range of different wills. This poses a challenge: can the organisation embrace these differences, providing the freedom for the diverse expression of wills, without losing its cohesion?

2. Understanding the Context
(The Work the World Wants Us to Do)

All organisations operate in a context, in the world. The context includes the civil, economic and political conditions and relationships at the local, national and global levels.

Organisations need to understand the various layers of the context they live in, both to identify the work that is needed and the conditions that affect their ability to do the work. In today's world the context is continually changing. What was true last year may no longer be true and so the members of a healthy organisation will continuously have to keep their eyes open and adapt to make sure that the work they are doing remains relevant.

Just as an organisation needs to know what it wants to do, so it needs to discover what the world really needs or wants to be done (and where). In discovering this, an organisation can match those things that it wants to do with those things that are needed. In this way, it can discover its true purpose.

CHAPTER FOUR: THROUGH THE LOOKING GLASS

3. Purpose — Marrying our Will to the Context

Did you hear the one about the horse-whip maker who hated motor cars?

KIKI TELLS THIS STORY...

Did you hear the story about the horse whip maker who hated motor cars? It may sound like a joke, but it really happened. One of the most successful companies in England in the early 1900s made its money from producing and selling horse whips for the drivers of horse-drawn carriages. They were proud, and passionate about their work — their mission was to be the best horse whip maker in Britain — but they had one fatal flaw. They refused to accept that motor cars were becoming more popular and affordable and that soon they would completely replace horse-drawn vehicles. As the demand for horse-whips disappeared, the company's sales dropped through the floor until it went bankrupt. Because they couldn't bear to face the fact that their product wasn't needed any longer, they were unable to make the changes that might have allowed them to diversify their activities and try to produce other products for which there was a demand. Blind to the reality of their situation, the great company died.

An organisation's purpose tells you why it is doing its work, why it makes sense, why it is relevant, given the needs of the world in which it works.

E.g. *Our purpose is to enable women affected by HIV/AIDS in Khayelitsha to support each other and organise themselves to access their rights, so that they may live longer, healthier and happier lives.*

Good purpose guides your work and it is against this purpose that you will be able to measure your organisation's contribution to change. A purpose should be inspiring and easily understandable by those who will be guided by it.

PASSION AND RELEVANCE

After the struggle against apartheid came to an end in the early 1990s, many NGOs were unable to adapt to the new and more complex realities that now existed in the South Africa. Some, still locked in defiant struggle mode, became increasingly irrelevant. Others, excited by the change, bent over backwards to serve the new government and in doing so lost their passion and their critical capacity, becoming little more than docile service providers to government. Because they lacked a clear understanding of what they wanted to do in relation to their new context, both groups were unable to refashion their purpose to meet the new realities.

What's the point of doing what you want to do if it's not needed? But is it any better to do something that is needed even if you don't really want to do it?

Neither is the way to go. Good purpose comes from the overlap of what you want to do as an organisation – the will/feet of your organisational identity – and your understanding of what the world needs or wants done. This is represented in the Organisational Elements and Cycles diagram by the overlap of two circles (p91).

VISIONS OR LEADING IMAGES

Sometimes it helps to have a strong vision, as an inspiring, purposeful picture of what you are working towards in many years' time. You have to be careful that this is not too fantastical (e.g. "We have a vision of 1000s of peer support groups across the country, a national solidarity movement and an HIV+ woman Health Minister in 5 years!"). But nor should you stop yourself being bold.

Some organisations prefer to create a Leading Image, which is a detailed, possibly bold, but realistic picture of where they want to be in 1 to 2 years' time. Such a picture helps to bring together and integrate everybody's ideas and desires, to really "see" the future together.

Some organisations, working in very uncertain and unpredictable areas, prefer not to have either, but rather to work out of good principles, values and purpose, staying open to a variety of futures as they emerge. But in whatever situation, purpose needs to be flexible as conditions change and as you learn more about what is possible.

CHAPTER FOUR: THROUGH THE LOOKING GLASS

4. Strategy and Approaches

FINDING YOUR REAL WORK

> An organisation's Core Approach tells you the organisation's deeper thinking about where the real work lies, the key processes by which it will achieve its purpose.

E.g. *Our approach is to help affected women to develop strong relationships with each other, for personal support, and as a basis for solidarity. On this foundation, we will help them to cooperatively build confidence in each other and knowledge that will enable them to develop a strong voice, solidarity, organisation and creative strategies to engage with the State, to access resources and services that are due to them. We will help them to continually learn from their own experience and deepen their own thinking to become progressively more independent of us.*

> An organisation's Strategy tells you how the organisation will translate their approach into action.

E.g. *Our strategy is to help peer support groups of HIV + women to form groups to counsel each other, from their own experience. We will identify HIV+ women through local day hospitals and testing centres, providing them with introductions to existing peer support groups. We will hold awareness raising processes with the groups to help the groups know their rights and to understand what avenues are available for accessing their rights (like grants, treatment, food parcels). We will also introduce support groups to each other to build a larger solidarity, based on horizontal learning activities, as a foundation for collective action. As groups get stronger we will increasingly take our direction from what matters to them, which may shift our activities to unknown areas.*

In our experience few organisations are conscious of their underlying approach to change and work in haphazard and unproductive ways as a result. (In the case of early pioneering organisations, this is not a huge problem, as they are intuitively experimenting with their work.)

Many organisations, following the Project Logic demanded by their donors, take their larger purpose and break it up into separate objectives and activities, e.g. Logframes, which they hope will all add up to achieving their purpose. Sometimes, if the conditions of change are simple and projectable, (as described in Chapter 1 page 20), this can work. But in most development scenarios they risk running a fragmented practice that does not generate linkages and new possibilities.

Taking time, now and again, to really think and rethink purpose, approach and strategy can bring real life and depth to an organisation's practice. This is where good planning, monitoring and evaluation cycles are critically important. By keeping focused and conscious of where the real work lies, you can avoid unthought-through activities, and save enormous time, resources and frustration down the line.

ORGANISATIONAL ELEMENTS AND CYCLES

A. ORGANISATIONAL IDENTITY
Principles and leading ideas (head)
Values, culture, relationships (heart)
Organisational will (feet)
What the organisation wants to do.

B. UNDERSTANDING THE CONTEXT
Civil, economic and political conditions and relationships at local, national and global levels.
What the world needs and wants to be done.

C. PURPOSE
Vision, mission or vocation

D. STRATEGY AND APPROACHES

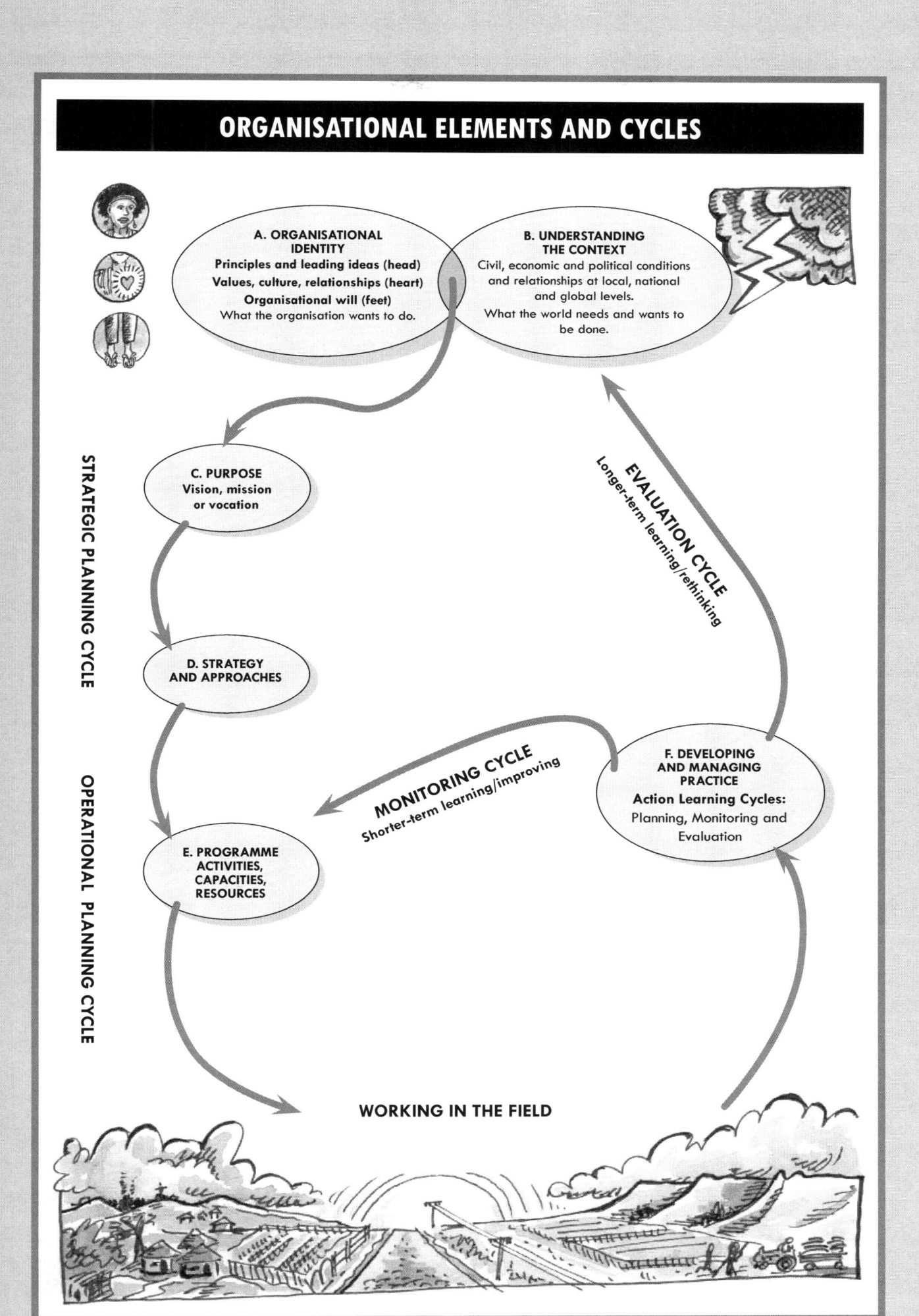

E. PROGRAMME ACTIVITIES, CAPACITIES, RESOURCES

F. DEVELOPING AND MANAGING PRACTICE
Action Learning Cycles:
Planning, Monitoring and Evaluation

STRATEGIC PLANNING CYCLE

OPERATIONAL PLANNING CYCLE

EVALUATION CYCLE
Longer-term learning/rethinking

MONITORING CYCLE
Shorter-term learning/improving

WORKING IN THE FIELD

CHAPTER FOUR: THROUGH THE LOOKING GLASS 91

5. Programme Activities, Capacities and Resources

This element encompasses the more visible working practices of an organisation. Once the purpose is clear, and once the organisation's approach and strategy have been determined, this element of the organisation tackles the task of formulating the activities through which the programme strategies will be implemented. At the same time, it mobilises the human capacities – skills, methods and techniques – that are needed to undertake these. Included here too are the physical resources and direct administrative support systems needed to support programmes, both in the office and in the field.

6. Developing and Managing Practice
(including the Action Learning Cycles - Planning, Monitoring and Evaluation)

Have another look at the Organisational Elements and Cycles diagram. Notice that this element connects to all the other elements through the Planning, Monitoring and Evaluation Cycles. These cycles are like the blood circulation of the body, continually feeding the organisation so that it can renew itself regularly and develop itself over time.

This element also represents the management of the other elements through learning processes and through systems and procedures – managing the people, the practice and the resources of the organisation.

Action Learning is the phrase used to describe the continuous cycle of learning in order to improve practice. All organisations learn and think as they go along, whether consciously or not, but effective organisations devote regular time and energy to it. See Chapter 7 for guidance and ideas about this.

ACTION LEARNING CYCLES

Planning, Monitoring and Evaluation are part of the larger Action Learning Cycle of the organisation. There are continuous cycles of planning, implementing, monitoring, replanning, implementing, monitoring and then longer cycles of strategic planning, implementation and evaluation.

PLANNING

Planning is a process that clarifies the intentions and purpose of organisations and links them to its actions. Planning has two components: Strategic Planning, and Operational Planning.

> **STRATEGIC PLANNING** takes the work done on developing the organisational identity and understanding the context, from which the organisation's sense of its purpose stems, and uses this to develop and to periodically rethink the organisation's approach and strategies. Where there has been a preceding evaluation, this informs the strategic planning process.

> **OPERATIONAL PLANNING** arises out of the work done on strategy and approaches. It produces plans for programme activities and the development of the required capacities. Operational planning is influenced by learning from ongoing monitoring, enabling regular replanning and improvement of work.

MONITORING

This cycle is the shorter-term continuous daily/weekly/monthly process of reflecting on your strategies, approaches, activities and supporting systems, to ensure that they are still on track and geared towards meeting your Purpose. It involves learning, re-thinking and re-planning. In this way, the organisation's work constantly adjusts itself and improves.

EVALUATION

This is the longer-term cycle of learning and re-thinking the work of the organisation, and the organisation of the work, based on experience and progress over time.

Evaluation draws learning from practice and measures the extent to which the organisation is actually meeting or has met its purpose.

The aim of evaluation is to assess how the organisation has supported programme work and and how it draws learning for future improvement. Evaluation thus enables a re-think of the organisational identity and a re-examination of the context, to see what has shifted. Any changes in the surrounding conditions need to be incorporated into a re-thinking of purpose, and consequently of the organisation's approach, strategies and activities.

A WORD OF CAUTION
to Donors and International NGOs

Conscious, organised and systematic PME or action learning may not be appropriate in organisations in their early pioneering phase. Young organisations learn huge amounts simply by doing. It is important for donors and facilitators not to encourage or pressurise early pioneer organisations to monitor, re-plan or evaluate too consciously or too thoroughly. This is a fairly unconscious time in an organisation's life, and, like early childhood, it is often marked by intuitive, experimental, trial-and-error learning and on-the-fly rethinking and re-planning. In some ways there often isn't enough experience yet for meaningful learning. Let them get on with it. When the need and realisation for a more conscious approach starts to emerge, then offer support, if needed, to help them grow their planning, monitoring and evaluation systems a step at a time.

LOFTY SHARES A FRUSTRATING EXPERIENCE

Once, a long time ago, I co-pioneered a small education NGO working with students and teachers on the Cape Flats. We applied to a few donor organisations for funding, and when we got the funds there was great excitement. But there were strings attached. The documentary requirements were so complicated that I found I was spending so much time on documentation — annual plans, quarterly reports, evaluations, briefings and so on, that there was hardly any time to spend on the real work of the organisatuion. What was particularly annoying was that each set of documents had its own format and needed to be serviced in a particular way. I suppose this was the funders' way of trying to ensure that we had a good practice, but their excessive demands had the opposite effect — it kept me out of the field, and prevented me from fulfilling the role that I should have been playing at that stage in the development of the organisation, undermining our practice.
It was extremely frustrating.

Donors must let pioneer leaders lead, in the field. They should be careful not to tie organisations up in red tape, long proposals, time-consuming reports, maintaining donor relationships and fulfilling bureaucratic requirements. This is one case where less is definitely more!

Using the organisational elements and cycles diagram to read an organisation

When organisations ask a facilitator to come in and help them with a particular set of problems, a survey is often the best place to start. Basically, the facilitator begins by simply observing and listening to the organisation. Our job is like holding a mirror to the organisation. The Organisational Elements and Cycles diagram provides a useful model that can help to develop questions to guide this process.

The facilitator begins by conducting confidential interviews with staff members, individually or in groups, and observing the people at work. Sometimes the facilitator will ask if he or she can participate in some activities, just to get a feel for the life of the organisation.

Facilitators are often asked to help with a new strategic plan or to conduct team-building or relationship work. Or they might be asked to help with restructuring, or to help in developing a monitoring and evaluation system.

Whatever the request, it invariably turns out that there is a lot more to the problem than meets the eye at first glance. For example, a request for team-building may arise because of a lack of cohesion or repeated conflict in an organisation. Through observation and diagnosis, the facilitator might discover that different groups in the organisation have different interpretations of its purpose of the organisation. This could well be a major source of conflict.

Sometimes facilitators are requested to do Strategic Planning because a plan isn't working, only to find out that there's nothing wrong with the plan, and that the problem lies with the organisational culture or relationships within the organisation. In this case, a new plan is not the answer, and will probably also fail unless the organisation's values, relationships and culture are revisited and renewed.

By making the organisation aware of these typical organisational elements and cycles, the facilitator can help the organisation to see itself better, and take action to implement a more appropriate way of working.

"Whatever the request, it invariably turns out that there is a lot more to the problem than meets the eye at first glance."

FOR MORE RESOURCES DON'T FORGET OUR WEBSITE:
www.barefootguide.org

CHAPTER FOUR: THROUGH THE LOOKING GLASS

TECHNIQUES FOR OBSERVING ORGANISATIONS

"Once trust is established, more intimate insights become possible."

Observing an organisation does not mean assessing or judging it. It's really about seeing and appreciating the organisation for what it is and what it is striving to be, rather than what it "should" be or how it compares with other organisations. In a field in which phrases like "best practice" and "world class" are continually bandied about, this can present quite a challenge! In particular, as facilitators, we need to put our own ideas about what a good organisation should look like to one side, and appreciate what we are looking at. It's not an easy thing to do. Even after many years of working with organisations, it's still a struggle to put aside our experience of what's good what's not so good, in order to refrain from imposing our opinions on others.

RUBES SHARES A HOMELY METAPHOR

Let me take you on a journey back to my childhood. I want to tell you about a special house that meant a lot to me. It was the house of a neighbouring family that I liked very much, and I spent a lot of time there. In the beginning all I saw of the house was the outside — but I still have a strong impression of its shape and size, of the neatly painted walls and their garden with its delightful flowerbeds. I can even remember exactly the kind of roof it had.

At first, the interior of the house was a mystery to me. I can still remember, the first time my Mom and I went over there, I got a quick peek into what lay behind the front door before my Mom whisked me away. The next time I went there I played with the kids in the back yard, and got a different view of the house. Then, the next time, I was invited inside for tea and biscuits and had a chance to explore a bit more. Each of the rooms said something about the family, the kids' chaotic bedroom, the homely kitchen, the living room with its comfortable old furniture. I especially loved the kitchen. The mother of the house loved to cook and the kitchen shelves were brimming with interesting stuff that we didn't have at home.

As my friendship with the family grew stronger, I began to spend more time with them, and I got to know every nook and cranny of that house. It became like a second home to me. Knowing their house so well gave me a much better idea about the family — how they lived, their likes and dislikes, and the things they believed in very strongly. For example, they always sat and ate supper as a family, always insisted that we washed hands before eating, and always began each meal with a prayer.

It would have been impossible to get to know this home so well without establishing a relationship that grew over time until I was a well loved guest who had the privilege of spending quality time with the family. Working with communities and organisations is like this. At first you are only able to see it from the outside, but as your relationships develop, so your view of the interior life of the organisation begins to expand. Once trust is established, more intimate insights become possible. As people begin to let you into their organisations, your knowledge of the organisation becomes deeper and more valuable. Clearly, building relationships and gaining understanding are intimately related.

Just as sight is only one of our senses, so the observation of an organisation depends not only on the obvious things, but on our ability to apprehend those aspects that are less visible or even out of sight. These include the relationships that exist within the organisation, its culture and so on.

The Phases of Organisation Development model and the Elements and Cycles of Organisation diagram are useful tools or windows to guide your questioning process. To make the best use of them, here are some techniques that will enable you to go deeper in your exploration of the stories, elements and cycles of the organisation. Bear in mind that these techniques should not be seen as separate, and should be used simultaneously.

OBSERVING THROUGH PARTICIPATION

Participating in all the different aspects of the organisation's life can often bring deep insight. This might include attending a team meeting, accompanying staff on a field-trip, or sharing a meal with staff members. It's quite normal for the members of an organisation to put on a show for you if they aren't used to having you around. Sometimes, if things aren't great within the organisation, some people might even try to hide what's really going on. The key is to be able to move beyond this initial stage, to a more relaxed situation where people feel freer to be themselves. For outside facilitators, participation can help you to get further under the skin of the organisation than you otherwise would.

Being a "fly on the wall" can be useful – you can try hanging around reception or where people have tea, to get a feel for how people behave and relate to each other. But be careful that people don't think you are snooping on them!

In Rubes's story about getting to know his neighbours, it was only when he knew them well enough to start sharing mealtimes with them that their beliefs and rituals became visible to him. Similarly, in an organisation, values and patterns of behaviour can be so entrenched and taken-for-granted that staff members are hardly aware of them. In this situation, asking questions isn't going to reveal much. Participation can help make the invisible more visible.

OBSERVING THROUGH QUESTIONING, LISTENING AND CONFIDENTIAL INTERVIEWS

In Chapter 2 we looked at questioning and listening as key skills for leaders and facilitators – in particular, how to listen to the Head, Heart and Feet. Leaders and facilitators can learn an enormous amount through confidential interviews – by asking people questions and listening to their responses. Such interviews can be conducted both with individuals or with small groups.

Confidential interviews can reveal key information or even secrets about the organisation. This can put you in the strange position of knowing things about an organisation that have not been shared amongst all its members. Your task is not an easy one – to maintain confidentiality while encouraging people to be open and transparent with each other.

"Being a 'fly on the wall' can be useful – but be careful that people don't think you are snooping on them!"

CHAPTER FOUR: THROUGH THE LOOKING GLASS

A Note on Questionnaires

- If you need to use questionnaires to get a consistent set of responses to specific questions then do make sure that you leave space for people to tell you things that are not covered by your questions.
- It may be useful to begin with questions that are open rather than specific, allowing the conversation to flow. Leave time at the end to check to see which of your prepared questions have not been answered.

"Encouraging people to find real experiences to back up their opinions can help them to re-examine their opinions in a new light."

Some staff members may be happy to share certain information with you as long as their names aren't mentioned as a source of the information. It is important that you try to verify anonymous information like this so that you don't become a vehicle for false accusations.

People are more likely to speak openly and honestly if you can create a safe atmosphere.

While interviewing it is common for people to skip over something which is uncomfortable but important – if you sense that there is more to tell you might want to say "could you say a little more about that, please." Often this simple prompt will lead to the most important information.

It is also a useful practice to engage with stakeholders outside of the organisation as well. These may be people who have particular perspectives of the organisation through its work. They may be part of the target group, partners and even government officials etc. This will help you to form a richer picture of the organisation you are working with.

OBSERVING BY SURFACING REAL STORIES OR EXPERIENCES

Whether in interviews or through workshops and group processes, people should always be encouraged to give specific examples from their experience. These experiences can then be explored to develop deeper insights. Encouraging people to find real experiences to back up their opinions can help them to re-examine their opinions in a new light. The section on Action Learning (Chapter 5) provides guidance for working with and learning from experience.

OBSERVING BY LISTENING TO FEELINGS

Feelings often give clues to hidden things that matter most to people. Helping people to express their feelings is thus a key technique for discovering what lies beneath the surface. If you can help people to express these feelings to each other it can provide a deeper path for facilitating change.

OBSERVING BY LISTENING TO THE WILL

Helping people to gain better knowledge of what they really want can enable them to understand their own behaviour better. Many of us have no clue what we really want, but are aware that deep down there is a need, an intention or a yearning.

Sometimes different people imagine that they want the same things as everybody else, but deeper questioning may reveal that in fact they want entirely different things. Conversely, people who think that their needs are different may find out that they want the same things as everybody else. Either way, if you can help people to surface and then share what they want, they are more likely to be able to find common ground and move forward.

OBSERVING YOUR OWN FEELINGS AND REACTIONS

Think of a first encounter you had with another organisation. Did you feel relaxed and welcome? Were you inspired or confused when hearing about what the organisation was aiming to do and how it went about its work? Our own inner responses, so often ignored, are often of vital help in reading and seeing the organisation we are encountering.

OBSERVING THROUGH AN OUTSIDER

As a leader wanting to know more about your own organisation you may worry that your staff are not telling you the whole truth. This is more than likely the case, and the best thing to do is ask yourself why. It may be that they don't want to hurt your feelings. Or they may be afraid of you. Perhaps they are angry with you but are afraid of their own anger, that they will embarrass themselves. It is common practice for leaders to ask trusted outsiders (like facilitators) to observe the organisation, to speak to the members and find out what they are thinking, feeling and wanting.

OBSERVING THROUGH IMAGINATIVE INSIGHT

Sometimes problems are too hidden or complex for our rational minds to see – this is where imaginative insight can help. Just as poets and artists are able to reveal the deeper side of human life through symbols and metaphors, so we can use images and pictures to describe things at a deeper level. It's not necessary to be able to draw well – sometimes a "word picture" will do just as well. For example, someone might say that a situation feels "like a train going down a hill with no brakes" or that "the relationships in this organisation are like grenades waiting to explode."

WORKING WITH IMAGES

Images, whether verbal or pictorial, can reveal surprising insights for everyone – and can also stimulate good conversation!

To explore and examine your own impressions, start by trying to come up with a good metaphor for where you're at. If, for example, while you are observing an organisation, an image comes to mind of a tray of ice-blocks, it could mean that the people you are dealing with are totally frozen, and need to be warmed up a bit. Alternatively, if the image of a bus speeding down a hill towards a huge inferno comes to mind, it is probably a good time to put on the brakes. Sharing these images with the people you are working with can really help reveal some underlying truths.

MAUREEN AFUMBOM, A VSO WORKER IN CAMEROON, SHARES THIS STORY

Learning to let go

Organisational Development is a new phenomenon to our partners in Cameroon. The organisation in question was an example of where the founder/director had all the power and took all the decisions. The staff and volunteers, and even the Board members, simply had no say in how the organisation was run. When the director came into the office, everyone had to stand up, greet him and recite the organisation's motto.

The director was quite resistant to the idea of externally facilitated organisational development, for fear that this would betray or expose him. But the Board, supported by some of the staff, thought it was a great idea. It would give staff members an opportunity to vent their grievances about the director, who so far had shown no interest in hearing what the staff had to say. However he was quite happy to listen to the beneficiaries, and was quite comfortable with the involvement of the beneficiaries in the organisation's self assessment.

To enable the organisation to have a sense of control and ownership, it was suggested they form an organisational development (OD) committee to be the driving force of this process. The director was a member of this committee. During the process the members of the committee were amazed to hear the beneficiaries talk about how much they appreciated the work of the organisation. After the self-assessment, the organisation could more clearly see what its challenges were and they also had a vision of where they would like their organisation to be in the future.

But the facilitator was impatient and kept on calling me to say that the process was too slow and that the staff and volunteers were always in the field carrying out other activities instead of concentrating on OD.

The facilitator was telling them that "this is what it is supposed to be" not taking into account the realities of the organisation e.g. resources, level of education of staff and volunteers, work schedule etc. The organisation became defensive, feeling it was being criticised. The director had an argument with the facilitator. The facilitator told the head of the organisation that he was violating OD etc. The head wanted to know whether the facilitator was a watch-dog or a facilitator. Eventually they could hardly greet each other.

We had to step in to help resolve the problem, though not directly with the organisation. We planned a separate meeting with the facilitator, reminding him of his role, and helping him understand that only the organisation can decide to make change happen. He could only help them see the need to change but could not force the organisation to change, as it could readily accept change only if it did not feel threatened. We helped him see that OD was not something separate from the daily operations and that his relationship was invaluable for the change process.

Later we had another meeting with the facilitator and heard of some significant changes. The director had invited him for a meeting with the staff to review the OD plan. I observed that they were now a little bit friendlier. They cracked a few jokes with us and the facilitator admitted that this had been happening from time to time so far.

Five months later, the director, feeling less threatened now, started delegating some tasks and also planning activities with meaningful participation of the staff and representatives of the beneficiaries. He marvelled at the contributions of his staff/volunteers. He started realising the potential they had. He said to me 'Maureen, I now see things differently. I used to wonder what will happen to this organisation if I die. I now see the value of investing in people and helping them learn. I will just let everything go. I never knew that some of my staff knew anything. I realize some enthusiasm in them now, though I have not changed their financial motivation.'

When we organised an exchange visit, he sent one of his staff instead of going there himself. Though the changes are gradual, I felt impressed with what I saw after two years of working with the organisation.

CHAPTER FIVE
Stepping into the unknown
Facilitating change in organisation

> *Not everything that is faced can be changed, but nothing can be changed until it is faced.*
> — James Baldwin

> *Reformers mistakenly believe that change can be achieved through brute sanity.*
> — George Bernard Shaw

HI I'M MANO...

You may have helped people to understand what's really going on in their organisation... but the point is to help them to do something about it! The ride can get rocky, like arriving at the rapids when rafting down a river. This chapter has some ideas for negotiating the rapids and a couple of life-jackets to prevent you from drowning. You'll probably fall in, believe me, but don't worry, you won't be the first - and there are ways to get back up!

> The managers and field staff described what seemed like two completely different organisations.

LOFTY TELLS THIS STORY...

Lying Dead in the Snow

Several years ago a facilitator was struggling in the middle of a very difficult workshop with a small NGO of about 20 people. The organisation was at war with itself, consumed by infighting and distrust between the managers and the fieldworkers. The director had turned to him to help resolve the conflict.

He had begun the process by asking people to share their experiences and understanding of the problems. The director and managers told their side of the story and the field-staff told theirs, while the administrative staff remained silent, as usual. There was no agreement on what the problems were. They were describing what seemed like two different organisations and always it was 'the others' who were to blame. Then the facilitator asked the staff to go away in their three groups, with crayons and flipchart paper, telling each group to draw a picture of the organisation, of the crisis situation.

Forty minutes later they returned. The managers wanted to show their picture first. It was of an apple tree with healthy fruit at the top and rotting apples at the bottom. This did not help and perhaps even reinforced the divisions. The field staff's picture was more interesting. It was an aerial view of a house with no roof and several rooms, but all the doors were on the outside, with none on the inside. This led to some discussion and they agreed that there were communication problems for which they were all responsible. Then the administrative staff showed their picture. The picture was of a lovely deer, lying in snow, with barbed wire wrapped around its neck and blood gushing out. It was dead.

The facilitator says he remembers feeling a sense of shock in the room. In that moment the organisation changed forever. It was a jolt to all of them to see the truth so brutally told, and by the administrators, all women, who had been so quiet. From then on the conversations changed completely as people became more honest and open to each other, and by the end of the day a way forward was found.

> **QUESTIONS TO WORK WITH**
> - What really happened in this story?
> - Why do you think that the drawing exercise made a difference?
> - Do you have any thoughts about the role of the administrators, as the most marginalised group?
> - What learnings or ideas does this stimulate for your own practice?

"It was a jolt to all of them to see the truth so brutally told."

Common issues in facilitating change

In working with organisations over many years, we have come across several identifiable challenges that organisations face. These are listed below. The reasons for these challenges are always complex and differ from one organisation to another.

RECOGNISING POTENTIAL

The biggest challenge, by far, is that many organisations are unaware of their own potential resourcefulness and creativity. Most organisations have a rich diversity of talent and experience, ideas and strengths of the people that have yet to be surfaced and harnessed.

SEEING OPPORTUNITIES

Organisations are often blind to the opportunities out there for support and collaboration, not spending enough time or effort researching and networking with others to discover what else is possible. There are competitive or territorial barriers between organisations that often prevent this happening.

QUESTIONS TO WORK WITH: As leaders or facilitators how can we help people to unlock the rich diversity and resourcefulness inside and between their organisations? (The last chapter has some good "horizontal learning" stories and ideas for this.)

STRENGTHENING LEADERSHIP (AND LEADERS)

Leaders often struggle to find appropriate leadership approaches and can become isolated. How does this affect the way they lead?

It is also important to realise that leaders are only one form of leadership. We can also find good leadership out of our team processes, especially our collective learning and strategising meetings.

QUESTIONS TO WORK WITH: What kind of leadership does the organisation need? Where are people showing healthy leadership that can be strengthened? Where is leadership unhealthy and ineffective?

RENEWING PURPOSE

Confusion around the identity, context and purpose of an organisation – organisations and the people in them change all the time, seeing themselves and the world differently as time goes by. Things out there are also always changing, the circumstances and the needs of the world. And so purpose needs to change to keep up with the times. People

> As leaders or facilitators how can we help people to unlock the rich diversity and resourcefulness inside and between their organisations?

inside the organisation need to regularly renew and deepen their collective understanding of the deeper purpose of the organisation.

QUESTIONS TO WORK WITH: What matters most to us? What do we really want to be doing? What is really needed from us? Where is the real work and purpose now?

LEARNING OUT OF EXPERIENCE AND INTO THE FUTURE

The work of development is exceedingly complex and the context is always changing. Few answers are given to us. We need feedback and reflection to learn our way into the future. This means that organisations can only stay alive to what is possible, and thrive and sustain themselves if they are continuously learning from their experience and innovating their practice and organisational support to meet the changing circumstances always coming towards them.

QUESTIONS TO WORK WITH: How are we learning? How can we strengthen and support better learning from experience? How can we ensure that we do it regularly, not as a luxury but as a life-giving part of the cycle of work?

BECOMING AWARE OF POWER

Power lives in relationships and if one or other side is unhappy with the kinds of power being exercised, the relationships can become unhealthy and dysfunctional and develop into crisis. Many people are unaware of the different kinds of power that they do wield and could wield. In Chapter 3 we described several of these.

QUESTIONS TO WORK WITH: What different powers do different people have? What kinds of power govern key relationships and behaviours in the organisation? Are people conscious of these? Are they functional and healthy? What kinds of power are appropriate for governing relationships at this stage of the organisation's life? How else could power be exercised?

UNDERSTANDING ORGANISATIONAL CULTURE

Where hidden rules and habits undermine relationships, or where the organisation says one thing but does another, you can be pretty sure that you're dealing with issues of organisational culture. The informal rules and practices of the organisation are often more powerful than the formal policies and procedures.

Often the problem has to do with competing sub-cultures, or different centres of strong and hidden feelings that people have about each other, within the organisation. These can be a problem, though not always: diverse cultures living side-by-side can bring good variety and healthy tension.

QUESTIONS TO WORK WITH: How can we make these more transparent? How do we reconnect to our core values or build new values on which to base our relationships and culture?

COMMITTING TO OUR PRACTICE

Every now and then the organisation's practice becomes unclear and is no longer shared and understood by all.

QUESTIONS TO WORK WITH: What is our real work? Do we all understand it clearly? Do we have a well thought-through approach and strategy that we agree on and are committed to?

CLARIFYING PROCESS

Where there is confusion around roles, or lack of clarity around responsibilities, we need to bring clarity. Clarity of roles provides individuals with confidence that they are contributing to the organisation. They need to know what each other's roles are in order to cooperate fruitfully.

QUESTIONS TO WORK WITH: What are the roles needed and who will take them? What are the main responsibilities of each of these roles?

ENSURING SUSTAINABILITY

This is always a challenge! Often our lack of finance or funding stems from a lack of the ability to convincingly present an organisation's purpose, strategy or capabilities to potential funders. Sometimes this points to a challenge to advocate for, collect or earn needed resources. There are hugely diverse sources of resources for social change work, most importantly the collective resourcefulness of people themselves.

QUESTIONS TO WORK WITH: How do we develop a convincing case for support as well as the confidence and creative strategies to win that support?

Stepping into change

Collectively accepting the need for change

Chapter 4 focused on "Understanding the organisation". At some point in the process it will become clearer to the organisation what the real issues, challenges and opportunities are that they need to work with. Sometimes this awareness grows slowly, sometimes it happens in a moment.

It is a key turning point in the process of change when the organisation **collectively accepts the need for change**. There must be collective consciousness of the issues and sufficient will to engage in a change process, before it is possible to proceed.

Of course they may come to the realisation that they're actually fine, in which case what they need is a celebration!

WHAT DO WE DO ABOUT "DIFFICULT PEOPLE"?

There are always going to be one or two people who just don't "get it" – they don't on agree what the issues are and resist the call for change, even upsetting those eager to get on with the job. Perhaps they are threatened, or simply quite happy with the way things are, or maybe they want to be noticed. How do we respond to people like this? Often our democratic instincts urge us to "take a show of hands" and over-rule them, pressing on, even if we leave them behind.

CHAPTER FIVE: STEPPING INTO THE UNKNOWN

> "difficult" people are more helpful than we realise.

But be careful here... Sometimes these "difficult" people are more helpful than we realise. Often they are playing a key role, testing the group, representing a hidden voice of caution, challenging the group to go deeper. These voices are often brought in awkward or negative ways but that does not mean they should be ignored. As a leader or facilitator it may pay to support the right of these voices to be heard, helping them to be expressed more clearly and positively. Ask people if there is not perhaps something worth listening to, a question worth considering. Give space to dissenting voices.

You will often be surprised at what emerges from this patience and respect for all voices. Not only does it help for some neglected and difficult issues to emerge (sooner rather than later!) but it also builds a healthy culture which will encourage hesitant, less confident people to find their voices and speak up.

DEZZY TELLS THIS STORY...

I was once involved in facilitating an organisational review of a regional programme in East Africa. The programme involved us travelling across the length and breadth of the country in a dusty, beat-up Landrover. The driver of the Landrover was an amazing guy. He knew a remarkable amount about the organisation, maybe because he'd listened in to so many conversations that had taken place in the vehicle during long road trips. He was able to share all the issues of the organisation, clearly and succinctly capturing the points of view of fieldworkers and leaders, and we listened intently. Later, in one of the workshops that formed part of the organisational review, he stood up and challenged his colleagues to name the problem that underlay all of the other problems facing them. But no-one dared speak. We asked the group to draw images of the organisation and it started to become a little clearer what the problem was. But still no-one would name it. At last the driver stood up again and, like a modern-day Che Guevara, he implored the group to have courage and speak. Still the room remained clothed in silence. We allowed the tension to brew in silence... until he could no longer hold himself back. He stood up and boldly named the person who was mismanaging the finances, while the weak leadership did nothing. The truth was now out and could be faced.

> DIFFICULT? WHAT EXACTLY DO YOU MEAN BY "DIFFICULT"?

The Dissident Voice

This is a clear example of a marginal voice taking the space and opportunity to emerge.

This may also point to the question of who we engage with – and the importance of engaging with all people, even if at first glance they may not seem important to the change process. If they are a part of an organisation, however humble their role may be, they have a right to be heard.

Moving into Change Mode

Three paths to choose from

In Chapter One we described three kinds of change in society, including organisations – **emergent**, **transformative** and **projectable** change.

Here we look at some typical challenges that organisations face when they are going through different kinds of change.

EMERGENT CHANGE CHALLENGES

Organisations going through emergent change are not in crisis, and are also not ready for any major changes or projects.

In the early Pioneering Phase of an (emerging) organisation we have to be careful, especially if we are outside facilitators. Pioneering organisations are in a *less conscious* state of change and are sometimes best left to experiment and stumble on their own, "by the seat of their pants". Pioneering leaders need to trust their instincts, to be bold and experimental. Donors need to be supportive but should not demand too much explanation. It's a phase of learning by doing.

As the organisation matures, in any of the phases, the need for a more conscious emergent change process may arise. In this scenario it may be that certain improvements, small changes here or there, could be made, or certain aspects could be strengthened. An organisation may benefit from becoming more conscious of its practice, to surface it, articulate it more clearly, and enhance it.

TRANSFORMATIVE CHANGE CHALLENGES

Transformative change challenges are common where organisations are going through a crisis towards the end of their Pioneering, Rational or Integrated Phases. The challenge is for the organisation to revisit its identity, and the way it understands its context. Out of these understandings, a clearer sense of purpose can emerge.

There can be either a **cold crisis**, where there is a pretence of normality but behind the scenes relationships and practices are deeply unhealthy, with suppressed conflict, or a **hot crisis**, where the problems are out in the open, with periodic conflict.

There may also be an external trigger, like a severe lack of funding, a change of government, or even government repression, war, civil unrest, etc.

PROJECTABLE CHANGE CHALLENGES

Projectible changes are able to happen when the organisation and its environment are reasonably stable and healthy, and where people themselves are confident enough to take on a significant change project. This is more than improving what they are doing. It involves taking on something new, of doing something that will "up their game". An example of this is opening up a whole new area of work, expanding to a new region, entering a significant collaboration or developing new PME or administration systems.

KINDS OF CHANGE

EMERGENT CHANGE

TRANSFORMATIVE CHANGE

PROJECTABLE CHANGE

CHAPTER FIVE: STEPPING INTO THE UNKNOWN

Facilitating Emergent Change

Action learning as a core process of emergent change

"By asking the right questions, they are able to connect people to each other, to bring to light what people have and can build on. This in turn builds relationship, community and trust and lays the basis for more conscious change and continuous learning from their own and their peers' experience."

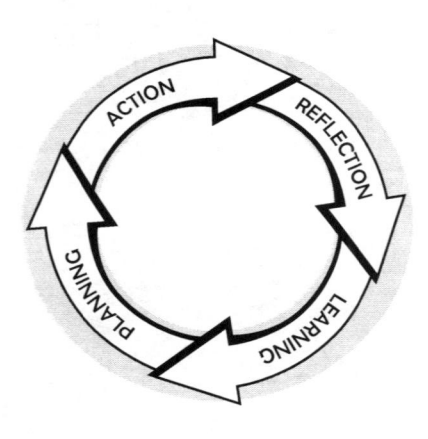

In conditions of emergent change the challenge is to work slowly and carefully, helping organisations to make conscious their relationships, their stories and their practice. To help people in the organisation to understand the emerging identity of the organisation, to grow and deepen their knowledge of themselves, their purpose, and their relationships, may be quite a process! It is very rewarding to see how, as they do this, their self-confidence and sense of sovereignty grows stronger.

Good leaders and facilitators intuitively work with emergent change when approaching or working with individuals, organisations and communities. They spend time connecting with the lives of the people involved. In this way, they are able to learn about what is really happening, or moving, on the ground. They are thus better able to understand what is possible, what's not, and what the stumbling blocks are likely to be. By asking the right questions, they are able to connect people to each other, to bring to light what people have and can build on. This in turn builds relationship, community and trust and lays the basis for more conscious change and continuous learning.

There are countless strategies and methods used by practitioners or leaders for approaching emergent change consciously. Many have the **action-learning cycle** at the core. As we have seen, this approach accompanies and seeks to enhance existing change processes and to surface potential, through continual learning.

Some methods often associated with emergent approaches include:
- participatory action research
- asset-based learning
- local and indigenous knowledge-based approaches,
- coaching, mentoring etc
- horizontal learning approaches (like community exchanges and other learning networks)

Horizontal learning approaches are becoming more common in the development sector. They show particular promise in cultivating collaborative learning relationships as a foundation for collaborative action in diverse circumstances. Many of the more effective social movements, in urban and rural settings, are founded on horizontal learning relationships and networks.

FOR MORE RESOURCES DON'T FORGET OUR WEBSITE:
www.barefootguide.org

THE ACTION LEARNING CYCLE AS A TOOL

Action Learning is a continuous cycle: the end of each learning cycle becomes the beginning of the next cycle.

ACTION

To do or experience and then recalling the experience: nobody knows your experience of your actions better than you do. To become more conscious of our "experience" while acting, can impact on the next step quite dramatically.

REFLECTION

Re-examining and thinking about the event or action means to make it more conscious, to analyse it, to evaluate it, to understand it better or on a deeper level. The problem is that we do not do this automatically. Often it is only as a result of a crisis that we reflect, that we stop to take a deeper look. A more pro-active approach is vital to become a good action learner.

LEARNING

Reflection is no guarantee that learning has taken place! Very often people "reflect" on practice and repeat the same mistake over and over again. Therefore the distinction between reflection and learning in the AL Cycle is important; learning here is the process of distilling or drawing out the core generalised lessons; moving from "what actually happened" to "what tends to happen as a result of such circumstances", surfacing deeper implications and guidance for the future. Be careful of jumping to learning before adequate reflecting has taken place, or the learnings will often be shallow.

PLANNING

This is the key link between past learning and future action (and learning). The core "insights" from the previous step must now be translated into decisions that will ensure improved practice. These decisions then need to become part of the plan. Planning that is unrelated to learning from the past is nearly always a waste of time!

The Action Learning Cycle

Guiding Questions

ACTION
What significant things happened? Describe the events. Who was involved, what did they do? What picture emerges? How did I/we feel?

REFLECTION
Why did it happen, what caused it? What helped, what hindered? What did we expect? What assumptions did we make? What really struck us? Do we know of any other experiences or thinking that might help us look at this experience differently?

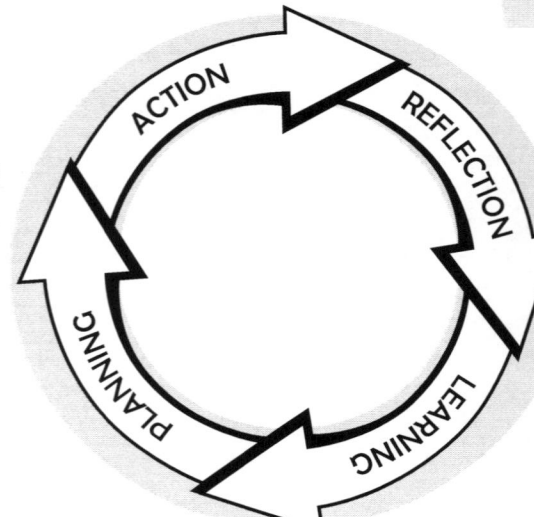

PLANNING
So what does this mean for practice? What do we want? What do we want to do, to happen? How? What are we going to do differently? What do we have to let go of or stop doing? How will we not repeat the same mistake? What steps will we use to build these new insights into our practice?

LEARNING
What would we have done differently? What did we learn, what new insights? What was confirmed? What new questions have emerged? What other theories help us to deepen these learnings? What guidance do we get for the future?

Facilitating Transformative Change

Changing identity from the inside out

Imagine the following scenario...

You enter an organisation. People are not talking to each other, the atmosphere is tense, there is a politeness that doesn't feel quite real.

There is a lot of talking going on in corridors. Gossip is very much a part of the organisational life, issues are personalised. There are differing points of view, camps and cliques forming around groups of people.

The leader is either isolated from it all or the subject of gossip, accused of siding with a particular group or person, or of favouritism.

The organisation's actual work is hardly spoken about. Conversations and time are spent on interpersonal issues, resolving conflict over sometimes petty issues. Small issues are blown out of proportion.

There is underperformance and low energy and morale or people are overworked and run off their feet.

A sense of pride is lost, the work is no longer exciting, projects are failing and funding is drying up. There is no sense of direction or clarity about what the organisation is supposed to be doing and staff are not sure what is expected of them or who is doing what.

This is an organisation on the verge of transformative change or of collapse.

CHAPTER FIVE: STEPPING INTO THE UNKNOWN

the U-Process as a core process of transformative change

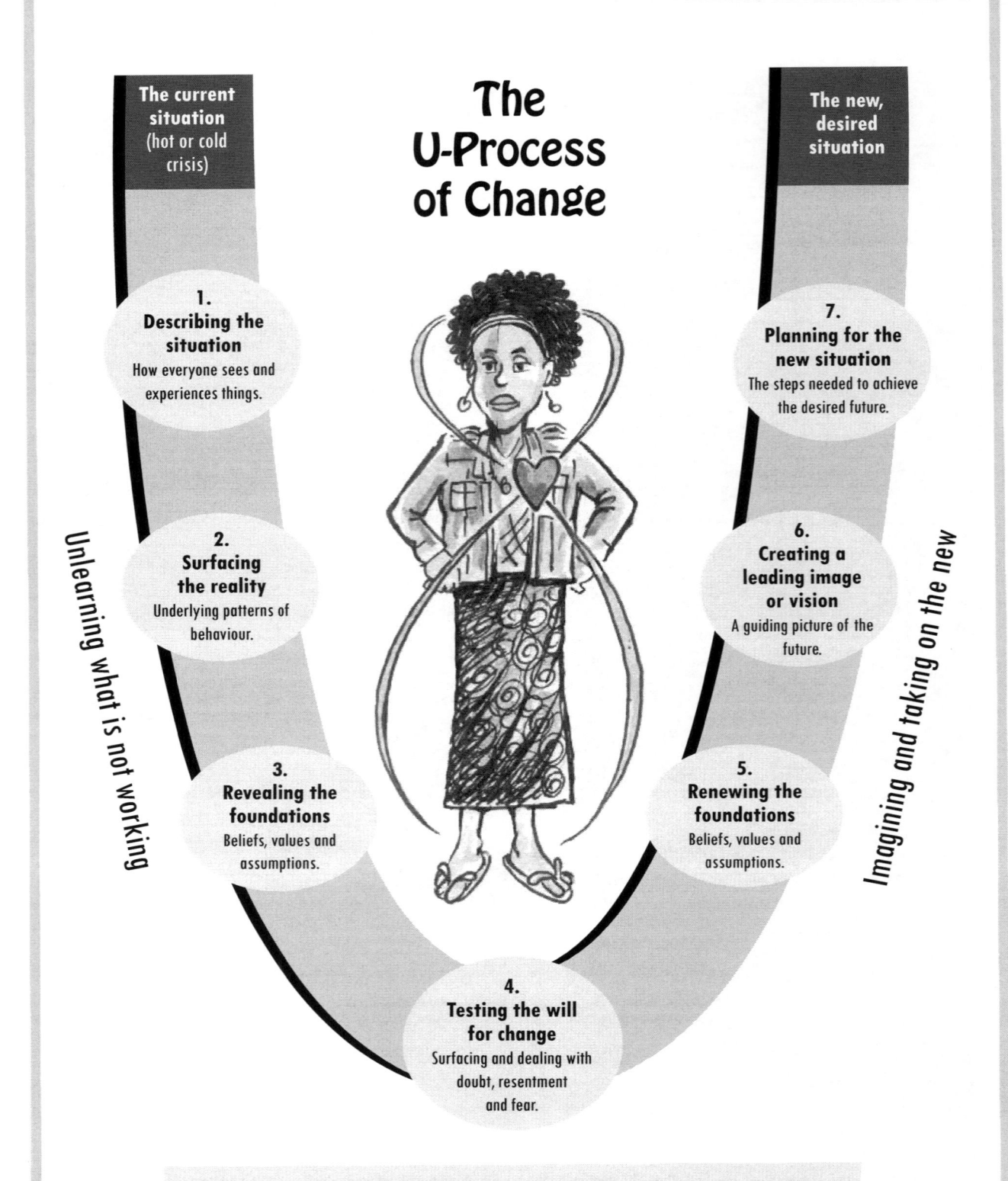

The U-Process of Change

The current situation (hot or cold crisis)

The new, desired situation

Unlearning what is not working

Imagining and taking on the new

1. Describing the situation
How everyone sees and experiences things.

2. Surfacing the reality
Underlying patterns of behaviour.

3. Revealing the foundations
Beliefs, values and assumptions.

4. Testing the will for change
Surfacing and dealing with doubt, resentment and fear.

5. Renewing the foundations
Beliefs, values and assumptions.

6. Creating a leading image or vision
A guiding picture of the future.

7. Planning for the new situation
The steps needed to achieve the desired future.

The U-process was developed in 1970 by Glasl and Lemson - (see Glasl, F. *Confronting Conflict: A First-Aid Kit for Handling Conflict*, Stroud: Hawthorn Press, 1999). A different but related version of the U-process has been developed by Peter Senge, Otto Scharmer, Joseph Jaworski, and Betty Sue Flowers. *Presence: Human Purpose and the Field of the Future*. Cambridge, MA, SoL, 2004. We still use the older and simpler version described here, but like the action learning cycle, the U-process is a change archetype that is as old as human development itself.

Transformative change processes are characterised by crisis. We cannot learn our way out of a crisis but rather have to *unlearn* our way through. What has to be unlearnt are the deeper attitudes, values, beliefs and assumptions that are the foundations of the crisis or stuckness, releasing the situation for new learning and *possibly* positive change. The example above illustrates some examples of unhealthy relationships, culture or leadership that would have to be let go of, to be unlearnt, before new life could take its place.

Transformative change approaches can be depicted as a *U-process of change*, as depicted in the diagram on page 112.

> Working with transformative change can only begin once the crisis or stuckness is ready to be faced — where there is sufficient initial will or acceptance for change, in the people and their leaders, to consider dealing with the problem.

IN A NUTSHELL... A conscious approach using the U-process will begin with the need for the crisis or stuckness to be surfaced and to be commonly understood by all involved or implicated. The practice here is of **collectively** uncovering the crisis, agreeing on what really causes it, letting these go and then creating a new resolved future.

The Seven Tasks of Working through the U-process

THE FIRST TASK — describing the situation

The first task is to get everyone to describe the crisis situation, to share their experiences openly. What has been happening? Get people to tell stories of the crisis, giving real examples of how each person has observed and experienced it, revealing their feelings as facts. Detail is important. Getting a full description of all the facets of the situation is important to create a comprehensive initial picture.

Do not proceed until everyone is satisfied that their experience is acknowledged.

THE SECOND TASK – surfacing the underlying reality

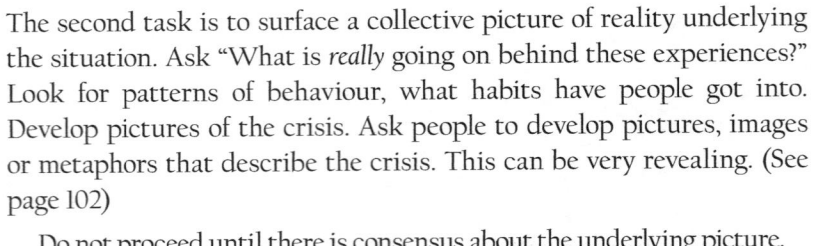

The second task is to surface a collective picture of reality underlying the situation. Ask "What is *really* going on behind these experiences?" Look for patterns of behaviour, what habits have people got into. Develop pictures of the crisis. Ask people to develop pictures, images or metaphors that describe the crisis. This can be very revealing. (See page 102)

Do not proceed until there is consensus about the underlying picture.

THE THIRD TASK – revealing the foundations

The third task is to reveal the foundations of the crisis. This is often referred to as the "attitudinal level". What are the underlying values, attitudes, beliefs and assumptions that explain people's behaviours? How do these create the patterns and habits described in the second task? This gets to the real foundations of the crisis.

This third task is always a tough discussion and requires people to acknowledge deep-seated views. Examples might be: "I have been overly competitive"; "I have not taken the women in this organisation seriously"; "We have not cared about people's personal lives"; "I have wanted to hold onto power because I don't believe others can do a good job"; "We are the best, we don't need to learn".

Through this process it becomes possible for people to let go of things that are not healthy or working, in effect by unlearning them. It is very empowering to be able to say: "I can see that holding onto these attitudes and values has caused the crisis we are in, and that it is no longer appropriate."

It is important to proceed with consensus. Remember that individual insights are not enough. What matters is that the group, as a whole, develops pictures and understandings that are true to them all, regardless of any blame or regret.

Of course some good values and attitudes will be revealed – not everything in the organisation is a problem or in crisis – and these should still be appreciated and valued. You don't want to throw the baby out with the bath water!

THE FOURTH TASK – testing the will for change

The fourth task is to test the will for change. Perhaps we can see the need for change and what has to be changed. But this does not automatically lead to change. We have to test the will for change.

This is the big turning point of the U-process, where the will for change is confronted and transformed. This is change at the Feet level. All the good work done up to this point will be incomplete and meaningless unless the will is also moved.

What often works here is asking each individual to spend some time alone asking these kinds of questions: "What do I **doubt**, in others and in myself? Who do I still **resent**? Do I **regret** anything I have done? What **fears** do I have of change? What will I personally lose if we let go of these things? What will happen if we don't change?"

Then the task is to give people an opportunity to share their answers to these questions with the group, one by one. Often just by sharing we realise that many others have the same answers and that we are not so far apart. So our doubts, fears and resentments become smaller and for most they become manageable or even disappear.

This task is critical, because without it there will only be a change of mind and of heart. The will must also change. As a leader you may be particularly challenged, possibly having to let go of some power.

Once the will for change has been surfaced and shared, you will have to ask yourself, as leader or facilitator, whether people are ready to move on to the next task. How will you know? It will usually become obvious by observing whether the mood and energy of the group has changed. If the process has worked you will most likely experience a sense of relief and a release of energy. People will start looking each other in the eye more, their bodies will be more up and forward, less slumped or dejected, they will be more sociable and chatty. If this is happening, let them enjoy each other's company for a while, informally, before moving on.

CHAPTER FIVE: STEPPING INTO THE UNKNOWN

THE FIFTH TASK – renewing the foundations

The fifth task is to renew the foundations. This task is a renewal of the identity of the organisation: "What core values, attitudes, beliefs, thinking or world view do we want as new foundations for the future?"

This is the other side to the third task. You are now helping the organisation to find new or renewed foundations for the new, resolved future it is creating.

One way of surfacing these is to ask the group: "After this organisation is gone how would you want it to be remembered? What did it stand for? What was important to it?"

THE SIXTH TASK – creating a leading image or vision

The sixth task is to create a leading image or vision.

"What do we want the future to look like?"

This is a creative process – encourage people to think out of the box, to be bold and imaginative. But it is also a real process – encourage people to be realistic. This is a difficult balance to hold, but one way is to say to people: "Think of this organisation in two years' time – imagine you can take a bus there and spend a few days with it... what would you see and experience?"

Begin by asking what areas of the organisation they would like to develop a vision for. And then ask them to be quite concrete and detailed when they develop their descriptions of the future. This way you are more likely to help people to see if they really do agree with the changes, not just of what they have to let go of, but especially what they are going to be doing together, and how.

Again, make sure that everybody is together – respect the difficult voices!

THE SEVENTH TASK – planning for the new situation

The seventh task is planning for the new situation.

"What steps must we take towards the new leading image?"

The new leading image or vision may be quite ambitious. Make sure that it is achievable, and that the organisation is properly equipped for the journey. But remember, getting there is a step-by-step process.

"Make sure that your vision is achievable, and that you are properly equipped for the journey!"

A WORD ON TOOLS

There are many different tools, models or exercises and most facilitators have their favourite ones. A tool is only as good as the thinking and approach behind it. Sometimes our favourite tools are not appropriate and sometimes we need to create new tools out of the situation and culture of the people there.

CHAPTER FIVE: STEPPING INTO THE UNKNOWN

Facilitating Projectable Change

The project-cycle as core process

> *It doesn't work to leap a twenty-foot chasm in two ten-foot jumps.*
>
> Anonymous

Essentially a Project is a well-defined piece of work, with reasonably achievable and predictable goals and with a clear set of steps towards achieving them. Projects require a degree of stability and predictability around them, both in their internal and in their external conditions, to ensure their success. If the conditions are not stable, the organisation may need to stabilise them, if possible, before proceeding.

For example, if there is conflict in the team or in the community, this may need to be resolved first, or if funding is uncertain it may need to be secured. Perhaps the organisation itself is emerging and can only handle small projects. If it is not possible to stabilise the conditions then either it is not possible to move ahead with a Project or a more emergent approach may need to be taken, proceeding one step at a time, perhaps with smaller projects, without over-committing, dealing with uncertainties as you proceed.

Throwing too much money at a fledgeling organisation can sometimes sink it!

MANO TELLS THIS STORY...

A donor gave a vibrant and successful community youth organisation, in a rural township near Cape Town, about $150 000, many times more than it had ever handled. This was for a big youth development project that we had largely designed (the community did not have the expertise) and sold to the community. Everybody got excited and got involved. Two years later the whole organisation had collapsed from infighting and the book-keeper was in jail.

Projects have a critically important place in development work, including organisational development. But Projects are deceptive – there is more to them than meets the eye. In a world where there is an urgency to deal with poverty it becomes very tempting for outsiders, be they governments or international agencies, with a mandate to "eradicate poverty", to cook up grandiose projects and deliver them to unsuspecting communities, via local organisations, whatever the conditions of change. These may even be preceded by wonderfully participative workshops to secure "ownership".

But the history of the development sector shows that this is a risky and often wasteful approach, as we see project after project failing for lack of real will or ownership.

But genuinely participative processes are possible using projectable change approaches. Consider this story from Cambodia:

> Genuinely participative processes are possible using projectable change approaches.

MEAS NEE, A DEVELOPMENT PRACTITIONER IN CAMBODIA, TELLS THIS STORY…

"All we do is aimed at helping people to begin to think for themselves again… Whatever action comes from their conversations about their problems, we support it. They are the ones who plan and think and solve problems for themselves. An idea will come up and in a few weeks time it will come up again. After a time they are pushing us to join with them to do something about it. Often an idea that begins like this becomes a Project which many of the village people join. So they move beyond numbness and a lot of options develop.

I find that the bond between people is more important than rules suggested from outside. When a Project starts I like the members themselves to come up with rules and the committee to decide on only five or six. Later when there is a problem and a way is found to resolve it I like to ask, 'Have we learned from this? Is there something else we can add to the way we run the Project?

The first thing is to make relationships, not to make Projects. The major goal of the redevelopment of the community is to help village people to regain dignity and unity."

TWO KINDS OF PROJECTS

- One kind of project is characterised by a **problem-based approach**, essentially identifying problems and seeking a fix. A broken tap is identified and a fix found. An organisational system is not working fully so the problem is identified and fixed.

- Another is characterised by a **creative approach** of people imagining or visioning a better future situation, not as a direct solution but as a new situation in which old problems are less or no longer relevant – a leap of imagination into the future.

- Larger programmes often need both.

This is particularly valuable when new work is suggested. Creative projectable change begins in the future, ie we project into the future, then plan backwards to the present, devising stepping-stones to the desired results. The stepping stones may veer between being tightly planned or loosely described as the people discover their way, guided and motivated by the vision they have created.

CHAPTER FIVE: STEPPING INTO THE UNKNOWN

Designing Projects...
beware of rushing into detail

OORS, A SCULPTOR, SHARES THIS INSIGHT...

If you were to take a piece of clay and try to make a little frog, for example, this is what you would most likely do: first you would imagine what it looked like and then you would squeeze and push the clay into something that roughly resembled a frog's shape. It would not be long before you started putting the eyes and mouth in and then you would work on the legs and feet. But then when you stood back you would see that it would not really look like a good frog because the overall shape is not there. You have rushed into detail before the overall frog-like shape is right. Yet if you then tried to change the overall shape, all the work you put into the eyes and mouth and feet would be spoilt and wasted.

We often do this with Projects. Why? Because we want to see the details, who does what, when and how, plus the costing – there is security and comfort in knowing the details. So we rush into planning the activities before we have designed the overall process, the bigger strategy. Some project planning methodologies, like Logframes, encourage this – after outcomes and outputs have been defined then activities are promptly listed in great detail. It feels very real and practical. But the missing step is design.

If the conditions of change are predictable and if we spend sufficient time on designing the bigger process or strategy, on its phases and stages, how this stream of work connects to that stream, understanding how the whole thing will unfold over time, then the details will become very obvious and be easy to fill in.

The Project Cycle

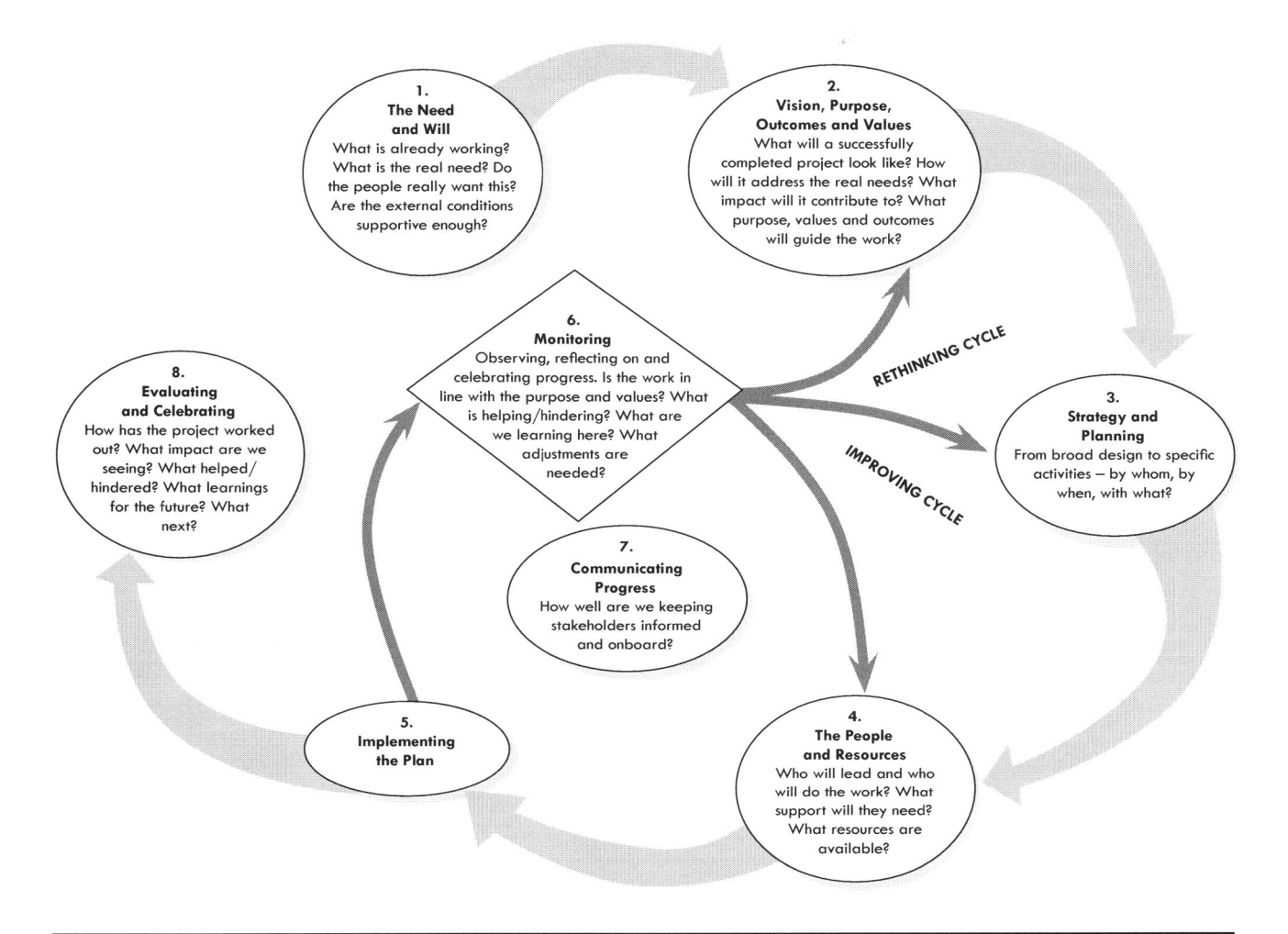

1. The Need and Will
What is already working? What is the real need? Do the people really want this? Are the external conditions supportive enough?

2. Vision, Purpose, Outcomes and Values
What will a successfully completed project look like? How will it address the real needs? What impact will it contribute to? What purpose, values and outcomes will guide the work?

3. Strategy and Planning
From broad design to specific activities — by whom, by when, with what?

4. The People and Resources
Who will lead and who will do the work? What support will they need? What resources are available?

5. Implementing the Plan

6. Monitoring
Observing, reflecting on and celebrating progress. Is the work in line with the purpose and values? What is helping/hindering? What are we learning here? What adjustments are needed?

7. Communicating Progress
How well are we keeping stakeholders informed and onboard?

8. Evaluating and Celebrating
How has the project worked out? What impact are we seeing? What helped/hindered? What learnings for the future? What next?

RETHINKING CYCLE
IMPROVING CYCLE

3 Key Challenges of the Project Cycle

PREPARATION

a) ensuring that there is a strong need and will that comes from and belongs to, the people involved;

b) the guiding vision and values. Investing time in collective processes of surfacing and developing the vision and values provides the invisible glue that keeps people working together – this is investment in the relationships that are vital for success;

c) investing in strategy design, as described above, before diving into the detailed activities.

MONITORING AS A LEARNING PROCESS

No project will be perfectly predictable and no plan can anticipate the complexity of what will actually happen when work starts. There will always be a need for action learning, for changing the plan as reality is experienced. It may even happen that the purpose and overall strategy of the project needs to be revisited sometime after implementation has begun. Project plans should always be seen as a draft.

COMMUNICATION

Because things will change, as a result of unanticipated realities, it is critical to keep all stakeholders up-to-date, whether it is the community at large, the donors or the trustees. This minimises misunderstandings and keeps expectations equal and thus helps to ensure that the conditions of change remain reasonably stable – essential for projectable change.

MANAS TELLS THIS STORY...

If your heart is in the right place … facilitative leadership

"You say he's been waiting for two hours and you didn't even offer him a cup of tea?" yelled the director of a grassroots NGO in Koraput, an impoverished tribal district. "But how would I have known that he was the head of our donor agency? He didn't tell me! He came by the night bus, and from the terminus by cycle rickshaw to our office. When I asked him about his work he said that he had just come to meet you. Nothing more, you know!" The office assistant was not at fault perhaps. Dressed in a pair of worn out trousers, a loose fitting Kurta and a pair of old shoes without laces and socks, Sriramappa didn't look the part of a funding agency head of the early 1990s. But as the head of OXFAM in Orissa, one of the poorest states of India, Sriramappa successfully facilitated a massive people's movement against the displacement of thousands of families due to the setting up of a Steel Plant. He also innovated ways to support a nation-wide movement of the tribal people for self-rule in their villages and hamlets. He facilitated a coalition of diverse NGOs to fight for rights over non-timber forest produce to be given to forest-dependent communities by cancelling a monopoly lease agreement with a privately owned company.

Sriramappa had understood well that to be able to bring people together you have to identify with them and walk by their side. To identify with people who have sacrificed their lives supporting struggles of communities, you need to be humble and value the significant contributions that the individuals that are part of people's movements have been making. International NGOs should not claiming credit for the support and contributions made. It is the genuineness of your efforts that matter and if communicated it works wonders in building solidarity and relationships. There's much that one can still do as an outsider to the process, like research, documentation, some reports, a little advocacy… But that's just going to be maintenance work. To make changes, you have to be part of the change too. If it's just your head that's in the right direction but not your heart and not your feet, you can write books about change, but forget about helping make them.

Drawing threads together

What is needed when we are leading or facilitating change?

> *If the only tool you have is a hammer, you tend to see every problem as a nail.*
>
> Abraham Maslow

By now you will have realised, if you did not know it already, that the practice of facilitating change is not a set of easy procedures to learn and to implement. Here are some broad guidelines to remind you of the essential work for a healthy change process:

- **Meet the organisation where it is** – your practice must adapt itself to the organisation's process and conditions of change. Too often facilitators have one approach, one design, one tool, one hammer, that they know well and use for every situation (whether it is Action Learning, Appreciative Inquiry, the U-process, a Project Cycle approach etc.) All of these are powerful designs but only if used in the right conditions.
- **Create a safe space to connect with people at all levels** – for all voices to be heard, all views to be expressed, and all ideas to be shared. Listen for the difficult and marginalised voices of people who experience and can see the deeper and more difficult issues that may hold the key for real change.
- **Listen to the head, heart and feet** – look for change in what people think, feel and want. Use your own thoughts and feelings to guide you. But be careful that you do not impose your will, what you want.
- **Seek guidance from people** – as a leader or facilitator there will be times when you are not sure what to do next. It can be empowering for all involved, to simply say you are not sure what to do next and to ask them, the ordinary members, what they think is happening and what ideas they have.
- **Build authentic community** – through helping the organisation to find new ways of speaking to each other, allowing for all voices to be heard, helping them to connect at a more human level beyond 'meeting procedure'.
- Always look out for what is working well and help people to see it – this brings balance and perspective to the problems people experience and brings hope and resourcefulness to the surface.
- **Develop and encourage shared and distributed leadership** – shared or collective leadership can happen through good meetings or action learning processes where decisions are reached by consensus. Distributed leadership is where specific leadership mandates are taken by different individuals, thus building up leadership experience amongst a wider range of people.

FOR MORE RESOURCES DON'T FORGET OUR WEBSITE:
www.barefootguide.org

CHAPTER FIVE: STEPPING INTO THE UNKNOWN

TRACEY SHARES THIS POEM WITH US...

The Facilitator

I spent a winter with them,
watching how they talked,
the way the director would turn
when asked a question;
the subtle order of tea and coffee.
They asked: 'When will we start changing?'
They said: 'Nice work if you can get it.
What is it you actually do?'

I smiled and shared their jokes;
I asked them what they thought they were,
animal, plant, mineral, machine.
At first they were hesitant and recited
the company line and spoke eloquently
of vision, mission, goals. No heart.
But one day over lunch a quiet secretary
whispered that they were an orchestra
only some of the instruments had been neglected
and most were out of tune.

I went along to a rehearsal and sure enough
    there were
broken strings, a battered flute,
a drum whose skin was torn.
And still I listened.

A board member waylaid me in the stalls.
'We are a ship,' he said, 'more or less sound,
but battered by the storm.'
I looked out of the window and truly the horizon
    was askew.

The woman who headed HR reminded me of the
    calibre of the crew
But the woman who made the tea said ' No-one
    speaks to me.'

I was the loom on which they wove the cloth
of their past, their present and at last their future.
I was the canvas on which they drew the cartoon
    strip of their progress.

I'd brought a bag of tools but, to be frank
I never opened it. They had their own,
unusual, but well-adapted
for use by musicians on a stormy sea.
While they patched holes and mended strings,
I was their temporary harbour.

For a while I was popular and enjoyed
a certain notoriety but slowly
they became absorbed in their own music,
plotted their own course. They were
so busy listening to each other,
they forgot me. I left them
sailing up the Amazon
playing a Strauss waltz
conducted by
the woman who made the tea.

CHAPTER SIX
Finding a home for change

Supporting, Grounding and Sustaining Change

> *We must embrace pain and burn it as fuel for our journey.*
>
> Kenji Miyazawa

HI I'M MUSA...

Change is more than an event — it's an unpredictable, back and forth process! This chapter offers an understanding of how to root change so that we do not slip back into old unworkable ways. We suggest ideas for creating a solid foundation for organisational change and dealing with the challenges found along the way. Enjoy!

RUBES REFLECTS ON A STORY WE KNOW ONLY TOO WELL...

Shortly after the first democratic elections of 1994, the new South African government embarked on sweeping reforms. Importantly, education would no longer be a tool of inequality and oppression, but a system that would liberate and prepare young minds to take their rightful place in society. Work was started almost immediately to introduce a new school curriculum which would transform the old system of Apartheid education and pave the way for change for generations to come.

A huge public campaign was launched and inputs were drawn from all walks of life. A Bill was passed through parliament giving rise to a nationwide initiative called Curriculum 2000. The launch of the new outcomes-based curriculum was followed by a nationwide capacity building drive. Many hundreds of subject advisors were

"More than 50% of schools in South Africa are now officially classified, by the education authorities themselves, as dysfunctional."

trained for months in the new learning programmes from grade 1 to 12, and in turn trained thousands upon thousands of teachers from every school, in the content, methods and values of the new curriculum. A phased approach was implemented starting with Grade One. Principals of schools were given advice and policy manuals on how to structure their schools to better accommodate the needs of the new curriculum. Teachers were now required to work in teams, the old subject formats were replaced with new learning areas and the assessment process completely overhauled. It was to be a thorough and comprehensive transformation.

This curriculum transformation was accompanied by three other big policy changes. Firstly, corporal punishment, abhorred by the new government, was outlawed at a legislative stroke (without much time or resources being dedicated to developing or rooting alternative forms of discipline in the schools). Secondly, 20% to 30% of teachers were retrenched to "right-size" schools in accordance with international norms and thirdly, all school principals had to devolve significant authority to new, democratic governing bodies of parents.

During this year (2008), the same students who pioneered the new curriculum twelve years ago, are writing their final school-leaving exams as young adults. Expectations are very low and widespread failures expected. A decade later the implementation of the "new" curriculum is widely regarded as being a dismal disappointment and the education system in the throes of a national crisis, including a breakdown of classroom discipline, teacher burnout and a higher than ever drop-out rate. A new cynicism has set in, accompanying the sense of failure and exhaustion that teachers feel. Many, even those from deprived areas, think nostalgically back to the bad old days. More than 50% of schools in South Africa are now officially classified, by the education authorities themselves, as dysfunctional.

> **QUESTIONS TO WORK WITH**
> - What really happened here?
> - What is it that makes it so hard for change (that is needed and makes complete sense) to take root and form part of how an organisation works?
> - How can these challenges be met more successfully in the follow-up and support of organisations?

FURTHER OBSERVATIONS

Such was the scale and pace of transformation in schools that it was felt that implementation had to be centred on mass teacher training, but the much-needed follow-up support to schools to coach and encourage them into the new system did not take place on the required scale, nor was it approached in a developmental way. The decisions and the plans for change were made, but the resources and support were not there to make it happen.

Sure enough, the new curriculum is embedded in more caring and developmental values, but the authorities have attempted to train even these into the teachers, as if these values were simple skills that could be transferred. What is more, the new values have not been reflected in the behaviours of the education authorities towards teachers – after all they had been similarly trained. Teachers are still being subjected to the same authoritarian management style of the previous Apartheid education department.

The new curriculum has been brought in on the assumption that what teachers already know belongs to the old system and they have been forced to learn a thoroughly new (and unwieldy) language and content associated with the new curriculum. Change has been taken so far that even what was working has been "transformed". The 'baby was thrown out with the bath water'.

The banning of corporal punishment, staffing right-sizing and the institution of parent governing bodies were themselves major transformation processes, indeed each a huge body-blow for schools to absorb. The scale and the pace of change has exhausted everybody.

Some learnings from this story

- Rooting and sustaining change is not a capacity building process that can rely on training and new policy manuals. Organisational transformation requires follow-up, encouragement, hand-holding, coaching, learning and unlearning, and a whole host of other support processes. Short cuts are not possible, no matter how great the need and determination. If these cannot be afforded then sustainable change simply will not happen.

- Change is exhausting – people talk about "change fatigue". There are limits to how much change people and organisations can bear before they become cynical.

- Whilst the stimulus for change (e.g. a new curriculum) can come from the outside, the change and transformation that matters is what happens on the inside, over time. Indeed transformation is both a relational and a psychological process. The plan had little understanding of the inner barriers that would have to be surmounted to enable teachers to take on the changes willingly.

CHAPTER SIX: FINDING A HOME FOR CHANGE

Why is organisational change so difficult to accomplish?

"Old ways of doing things are often extremely resilient."

Supporting, grounding and sustaining change is that part of a change process where things have to be firmed up, so that the change can find a secure place to live. We are interested here in those aspects of an organisational change process that will enable change to actually take root and grow, to mean something beyond the decision to change and the plan to make it happen.

RESISTANCE TO CHANGE

The old ways of doing things that are no longer useful to the organisation are often extremely resilient and won't allow the new to easily establish itself. In fact, resistance always tends to accompany a change process. Is resistance good or bad? We have to be careful about judging resistance, rather seeing it and accepting it as a fact of life. We could even see resistance as a vital part of change, not as something bothersome to be overcome; a challenge that, if faced and met, makes it more likely that real change will result. If you do not encounter any resistance when pursuing significant change it may mean that it is hidden and could emerge later to bite you, or it may mean that people don't really care whether things change or not.

People who are resistant to change may also have very good reason – perhaps they are seeing and experiencing things in the change that others need to be aware of. Until these are appreciated or heard it is common for people to resist and pull the organisation back.

> It seems that resistance always accompanies a change process. Is that good or bad?

> In my experience when resistance is surfaced, acknowledged and addressed, not only does it improve the change process, sometimes significantly, but it leads to an increase in commitment and energy for the work.

> Resistance can be healthy and when faced can bring good energy.

> Unless we resist the resisters!

THE EFFECT OF TEMPERAMENTS

In Chapter Two we described the Four Temperaments. Each brings particular challenges and contributions to change processes:

- The Fire temperament is often impatient for change, and is willing to take risks. This can bring good energy to the change process but it could also endanger it if the risks are too great.
- The Water temperament will often accept change but may hesitate and even appear resistant. It is likely that they are waiting for the right time to act, looking for the easy way through.
- The Air temperament loves change and brings a sense of optimism, without giving a lot of thought to how or why it is needed. Too much of this can be very risky, but people with lots of this temperament contribute much needed positivity and hope to the process.
- The Earth temperament is cautious about change and needs a lot of convincing. They can be overly pessimistic but their concerns are often misinterpreted as destructive negativity. They may be seeing obstacles and have questions that are worth paying attention to, saving a lot of trouble down the line.

Each voice has something to contribute. As a leader or facilitator working with a diverse group of people, expect, encourage and respect each of these voices. If they do not appear on their own then see if you can dig them out. Create opportunities for the impatience, the doubts, the eagerness, to be heard.

FROM DEPENDENCE TO INDEPENDENCE

At some point people want to take on the change process themselves, without facilitators. Indeed this may be a sign that we are succeeding. It may be that the change "event" has done enough and that people can take it forward now without further leadership or facilitation. But it may also be that, despite their new found direction and confidence, they may struggle to implement the changes without some support.

> We have found that once the significant breakthrough is reached, organisations often detach themselves from us as the facilitators, as if the main work has been done, and seek to find their own way into implementing the decisions they have taken in the process we have facilitated. Sometimes there are cost considerations but we wonder whether or not they have had enough of our help and the leader wants to get back to leading.

STUBBORN PATTERNS OF BEHAVIOUR

Even if the change process and plan is well formulated and supported, it is common for organisations to slip back into their old habits and stubborn patterns of behaviour. We all know that this is true for life in general, and no less so for organisations trying to change. We can even shift back into old ways without even realising it. It takes consciousness, reminding and practice to coach ourselves into new patterns of behaviour.

"One of the ideas that they all agreed on was to start using 'practice journals', in which they would record what they did while in the field, including their reflections and learnings."

MUSA SHARES THIS CASE STUDY...

Nice idea… but an old habit dies hard.

Two committed field-workers for a land rights organisation have for some years been going on field-trips, working with communities trying to regain their land. They have become very used to de-briefing each other during the long car trips home, chatting about the people they have met, going back over what happened and sharing impressions and learnings and what they might do differently next time. This has served their own practice perfectly, a very easy and natural "planning, monitoring and evaluation" system and as a result they have become increasingly effective over the years.

At some point the organisation, with the field-workers' willing participation, decided to become more systematic and collaborative in its learning process so that the experience from the different fieldworkers could be shared more widely and feed into new practice development and research processes. One of the ideas that they all agreed on was to start using "practice journals", in which they would record what they did while in the field, including their reflections and learnings. The idea was to use the journals as a basis for sharing and contributing to the practice of others. The journals were bought and handed out before the next trip.

But the two fieldworkers had become so used to their informal and effective car reflections that somehow they always forget to use the journals, and when they did remember, they just wrote the briefest of notes. They continued to rely on their informal chats, but when it came to practice reflection sessions, held a month or two down the line, they found that they had lost the interesting detail and could only share superficially with others.

QUESTIONS TO WORK WITH
- If this was your organisation, can you think of what you would have done to support or encourage the fieldworkers to really make an effort to use the practice journals when the idea was first accepted? What would you do now?

Managing the transitions of transformative change

> *The process of transformation is essentially a death and rebirth process rather than one of mechanical modification.*
>
> William Bridges

In Chapter Five we introduced the U-process which spoke about the need to unlearn attitudes, values, assumptions etc. that are holding us back, or keeping us in crisis. Doubts, fears and old resentments have to be surfaced and faced. This creates the conditions for new change to be born. But as the planned changes start to be implemented there may continue to be lingering doubts and fears, and residues of old unhelpful values, attitudes and habits. These will continue to exert some influence over the change process and may have to be re-surfaced and given some attention.

William Bridges has named this varying period of time between the old and the new as a *transition*.

WISE WORDS FROM WILLIAM BRIDGES

[We] imagine that *transition* is just another word for *change*. But it isn't. *Change* is your move to a new city or your shift to a new job. It is the birth of your new baby or the death of your father. It is the switch from the old health plan at work to the new one, or the replacement of your manager by a new one, or it is the acquisition that your company just made.

In other words, *change* is situational. *Transition*, on the other hand, is psychological. It is not those events, but rather the inner reorientation and self-redefinition that you have to go through in order to incorporate any of those changes into your life. Without a transition, a change is just a rearrangement of the furniture. Unless transition happens, the change won't work, because it doesn't "take." Whatever word we use, our society talks a lot about change, but it seldom deals with transition. Unfortunately for us, it is the transition that blind-sides us and is often the source of our troubles...

Bridges states that transitions are composed of three stages:

1) *an ending,*
2) *the neutral zone,* and
3) *a new beginning.*

CHAPTER SIX: FINDING A HOME FOR CHANGE

1. AN ENDING

Over time the people grow accustomed to and comfortable with set patterns in their organisation. The big challenge therefore in the ending is to let go, so that new space is created for the new beginning to grow and develop. This is never easy, and we cannot assume that the change event by itself can be enough to help people to let go.

It is important to realise that the old ways, even though they may not be useful anymore, were not all bad. In fact they may have served the organisation very well in the past, performing an important function in response to the needs of the time. Some people who were closely associated with past ways may feel that letting these go is a criticism of them, of their past work. This can create problems for how they engage with future change. Ensuring that their past contributions are acknowledged and celebrated can help them to let go.

Practically this stage may involve regular meetings, where the change process is reviewed. People could be encouraged to reflect on what old habits, practices, attitudes etc. are still being held onto despite an earlier commitment to let go. It would be important for people to realise that this holding onto the past is quite natural and expected, and that it will take effort to put them aside.

It may become important to create spaces for the past to be mourned. In many cases change events can be quite harsh, with staff cuts and loss of status in response to new job descriptions or appointments. When change is particularly drastic it may be helpful for the leadership to arrange a symbolic event where the organisation is helped to celebrate the past and put it to rest, not unlike a funeral ritual or memorial service in the case of loss of a loved one. Symbolic gestures like this offer a psychological avenue for helping us to let go.

2. THE NEUTRAL ZONE

But this letting go of old and familiar ways of doing things will still not translate into the new beginning that the organisation is trying to achieve. There is a period "in-between", through which the organisation still has to find its way. This is called the neutral zone. This is when the messy and confusing reality of change starts to kick in. A staff member may have to report to a different person and the new role expectations may not yet be that clear. People may lack new skills required for their new roles. Some consequences of change may not be fully anticipated, creating insecurity and frustration among the staff. This can also lead to some staff members leaving the organisation, creating even more uncertainty and even resentment felt by those left behind, who have to pick up their load. Productivity is likely to drop and this may set off great anxiety.

The neutral zone can be a chaotic time for the organisation. Bridges continues:

> The neutral zone is a very challenging point in the transition of an organisational change process. It demands patience, and ability to reassure and maintain calm on the part of the leadership, teamwork and lots of communication. This, accompanied with clear goals and a good plan to get there, will give the change an opportunity to settle and ultimately deliver on the promise that it holds for the organisation's future or the new beginning.

William Bridges

FOR MORE RESOURCES DON'T FORGET OUR WEBSITE:
www.barefootguide.org

However, it is also a very creative time, where seemingly insurmountable problems can be solved in unexpected ways. This period of confusion is also a time of opportunity for the organisation to experiment with new ways of doing things, a space for innovation. It takes the emptiness of the neutral zone to unlock this potential.

3. A NEW BEGINNING

The transition must end with a new beginning, a revisiting of the vision. This must not be done prematurely, before the old is dead and buried, before the strong attachments of the past have been loosened and remain just memories. The new vision will never be 'a road to Damascus' experience where we all become single-minded Pauls. Factions and opposition will continue, but hopefully re-defined and engaged in more constructive dialogues. The vision, mission and new strategic direction must be given shape and body by the staff, it must be believed in as worthy of commitment.

CHAPTER SIX: FINDING A HOME FOR CHANGE

Practical suggestions for leaders in implementing change

- If you are part of the leadership, consider taking the rest of the members into your confidence about the challenges and dilemmas of change, inviting their suggestions.

- Remember to build in frequent review sessions. These processes are extremely important to provide some certainty and security during a time that can be quite chaotic. These review sessions can be built into an already existing rhythm like weekly or monthly meetings for members. The action learning process is also a good tool to use for many different processes to build an accurate picture of an ever changing situation and make the necessary adjustments to the plan. Sessions like this can help to chart a sensible course through chaotic times.

- Allow people space to ventilate their feelings to help diffuse some of the tensions that usually accompany a transition and to surface emotional depth.

- Sometimes a representative "change team" can be very helpful. Different programmes or sections could be asked to put forward a trusted colleague to represent their voices during the process and through whom to communicate progress and challenges.

- People may have anxious questions about the change and if their leaders do not respond they will find answers from someone, somehow. But they may not be the right answers. The importance of communication during transition cannot be emphasised enough. It should be frequent and involve all the members. This helps to deal with some of the gossip and rumours that are inevitably part of the natural resistance to change.

- Seek an outside sounding board. Leaders from other organisations who have had similar change experiences are ideal counsellors.

- Don't push change too quickly. Have big visions, but don't hurry. Take small steps and bring everyone with you.

- Be guided by your values, principles and purpose.

- Remember to celebrate each achievement.

CHAPTER SEVEN
Staying alive to change

Learning and Innovating Organisations

> *In times of change, the learners will inherit the earth, while the learned will find themselves beautifully equipped to deal with a world that no longer exists.*
>
> — Eric Hoffer

> *We make the path by walking it.*
>
> — African proverb

HI I'M CRISSY...

If we want to sustain the benefits of change and keep things alive, then we may need to invest in learning, becoming more of a learning organisation. In this chapter, we will look at what it takes to do this, looking at both individual and collective learning, as well as how to breathe life into planning, monitoring and evaluation processes. We will also explore some ideas and stories about "horizontal learning" as a lively platform for new kinds of organisation and collaboration.

THE TREATMENT ACTION CAMPAIGN (TAC)

The TAC is the largest national social movement in South Africa. Through relentless campaigning, the TAC has successfully pushed the government to widen access to anti-retroviral drugs. The driving force has come mainly through the agency and mobilisation of people living with HIV and AIDS. The TAC has, through its campaigning, taken advantage of and used new political and legal spaces created in post-apartheid South Africa.

"When I walk into TAC offices it is like a liberated area. It reminds me of a candle and an open door."

KAMA TELLS WHAT IT'S LIKE TO WORK FOR THE TAC...

I joined the TAC in 2001 when I was at school. Comrades from the TAC Branch in Site B, Khayelitsha, came to visit us to get us to join, though it was banned at the school. This did not worry us.

The TAC has lots of youth cultural events and the songs really bring us together because when someone sings a song and we join them then it explains why we are really here. People add verses and the song and the message grows.

In the TAC we are given a chance to play a role, each one of us. There is trust and love and freedom. When I walk into TAC offices it is like a liberated area. It reminds me of a candle and an open door.

Though you won't see it we are sometimes messy and disorganised but its OK because we are all together. We have lots of different thinking, especially amongst the youth. We are mostly volunteers and some full-time coordinators.

The Head Office has asked each Branch to meet every Friday afternoon to share what has happened and plan. We share a lot. We sit and we share. We always start with a song and a game and then one by one we share whatever, but we don't force experiences. We say what we did, what went right and wrong and we try to fix these. Each one of us carefully writes down what was said to tell those who were not there. The coordinator writes a short report for Head Office. When we plan we go with the mood of the people. We really enjoy the meetings. TAC provides bread and tea and sometime a little transport money.

In the TAC we stay alive and connected. It is a community centre. The spirit is fire, warm.

> **QUESTIONS TO WORK WITH**
> - What strikes you in this story?
> - How important is the culture of the TAC to the way it is organised?
> - How would you describe the learning culture?
> - Practically how does the organisation learn and how important is this to the life of the organisation?
> - What do you learn from this that might be useful for your organisation or practice?

A LEARNING RHYTHM

Kama's story illustrates something very crucial – how it is possible for effective organisation to lie not primarily in efficient systems, but in human, even somewhat disorganised simplicity. What the TAC branches lack in sophisticated structures is more than compensated for by inclusive and accessible processes and sheer commitment.

The TAC has a learning rhythm: every Friday it meets and reflects, learns and plans, as much part of its work as any other aspect. And they meetings are enjoyable!

At one level there is nothing remarkable about this, after all, organisations meet. But at another level it is remarkable that it can be quite simple, and simply human – here an organisation, in every branch, gathers itself together, every week to think about itself, to re-form and re-think and re-ignite itself... and to enjoy being together. Its meetings are also cultural occasions, unique to itself, starting with a song and a game, a prayer, a time of camaraderie. It shares its own stories and thinks about them. No great technique here. And that is the point. It does not need impressive learning or knowledge-management systems designed by a consultant. Everybody is responsible for gathering evidence, learning and documentation. Indeed its slight messiness and disorganisation probably enables more participation and an emergent quality, in looser, human spaces, and an atmosphere of shared freedom, in which all individuals feel at home and valued enough to bring their diverse contributions.

And all of this makes possible a wonderfully powerful orientation to planning, to quote Kama: "When we plan we go with the mood of the people."

"It's slight messiness and disorganisation possibly enables an emergent quality, in looser, human spaces, and an atmosphere of shared freedom, in which all individuals feel at home and valued enough to bring their diverse contributions."

CHRISSY REMEMBERS THE STORY OF THE WOODCUTTER...

"TO PUT IT BLUNTLY..."

Once upon a time an old woman was walking through the forest near her home when she came across a man chopping down a tree. They exchanged brief greetings but he continued chopping. He was working very hard, determined to complete the job and see results before sundown. She watched him a while and then disappeared. A little later she returned, bearing a stone and a small bucket of water. When he paused in his work to wipe his brow she handed these to him and said, "Sir, I see that you are very busy. But, to put it bluntly, it looks to me like you need to pause a while, take a breath and sharpen your axe."

"Go away, woman, I am too busy I don't have time for this!"

When do we sharpen our own axes? When do we invest in learning, in improving and rethinking what we do. How many of us are also just too busy?

What does it mean to be a Learning Organisation?

"It's about an organisation that nurtures itself..."

The idea of a "Learning Organisation" has been around for a while now. All organisations learn whether they realise it or not, because the people inside them are learning - but like people, not all organisations learn well. To be a *learning organisation you have to try to be one*, to make an effort to learn consciously and regularly, to set quality time aside for learning. Having the right attitude is not enough... you have to do things differently!

A quick definition to get us going...

> A learning organisation deliberately puts regular time aside to learn from its experience, to think about what this means for practice and to develop its capabilities, in order to continually improve the quality of its work, to rethink its purpose when necessary and to strengthen how it organises itself to do the work.

It's about an organisations that nurtures itself...

The rule of thumb is that we need to put aside 15% of organisational time for learning – some may call this research and development.

SO WHY IS IT IMPORTANT TO BE A LEARNING ORGANISATION?

...Because we need to be alive to change

Just think about how things seems to change every day, every week, every month! Last year seems like 5 years ago! Conditions in many communities are deteriorating, prices are rising, the climate is changing, diseases and crime are up, our children are so different from what we were, the internet is changing the way we communicate, old jobs are disappearing and new ones appearing, new ideas and new initiatives are popping up all over... the list goes on and on.

If we don't try to stay ahead of the changes we will soon fall behind. A learning organisation, through rigorous and regular processes, looks around to see what is changing and thinks about what it is doing and where it needs to change, to stay on top of things.

...Because we need to be honestly accountable to each other and the world

Working with social change, whether as a leader or facilitator, requires a sense of responsibility. Change is a complex business, sometimes a life and death process, so we can't run around doing whatever we feel like – we have to be accountable, to understand whether what we are doing is helpful or harmful. In our experience the only way to do this in a meaningful way is to adopt an honest learning approach, to provide a true reflection to the world of who we are and what we do.

...Because the world is really complicated and we all need to try to make sense of it!

The causes of poverty and exclusion are far from simple – they are surprisingly complex and mostly hidden from the casual observer. The text-books and experts with degrees don't seem to have the answers. So people like you, people doing the work to improve their own and each other's lives, need to join the search to find answers, through learning from your own experiences AND the experiences of others. If we pool our experiences and learnings, through the organisations we belong to, we are far more likely to contribute to making sense of the world.

> If we want to democratise the world we have to democratise learning. Helping ordinary people to learn about the world and how to do things better to improve their lot, is a fundamental condition for change.

CHAPTER SEVEN: STAYING ALIVE TO CHANGE

"If we want to democratise the world we have to democratise learning."

...Because if we don't then the power will always belong to the rich and powerful who do invest in learning

Make no mistake, the rich and powerful invest huge amounts of time and money in learning, in research and development, in order to find new ways to look after their own interests. If we want to democratise the world we have to democratise learning. Helping ordinary people to learn about the world and how to do things better to improve their lot, is a fundamental condition for change.

Designing our own approach to learning in organisation

> **ARE THERE ANY "BEST PRACTICES" FOR LEARNING ORGANISATIONS TO FOLLOW?**
>
> This is a tricky issue. Many organisations have developed "good practices" for learning, and many of them could be the best in its own situation. We can learn much from healthy learning organisations and communities, but organisations need to develop their own approaches and practices. They may borrow and experiment with ideas from here and there, but not to try to become a replicated carbon copy of some "best practice" model.
>
> Each organisation has a unique way of working and learning and must be allowed to be unique if it is to be creative and successful

Just as there are diverse organisations, so there are diverse ways of learning. Each organisation needs to experiment with and work out what kind of learning approach and practices will best support, improve and challenge its work.

In order to design you own learning approach it will help to understand more about learning itself

LEVELS OF LEARNING

There are different levels at which we can learn, as individuals, as teams or as organisations. It is important to pay attention to each level when we design learning activities in organisations. See Chapter Two page 29.

HEAD LEVEL LEARNING

This involves acquiring and developing facts, knowledge and ideas. Two key challenges are asking good questions and thinking in creative ways.

HEART LEVEL LEARNING

Here we develop a range and sensitivity of emotions, and our capacity to feel, to empathise, to be sensitive to the attitudes and ethics that we value and that guide our thinking and doing.

FEET/HANDS LEARNING

This means developing and unearthing the skills, capabilities and also the will behind doing (e.g. courage, enthusiasm, confidence). Enabling learners to connect head and heart learning with action, with practice, to practicing. Helping learners to unblock their will, to deal with things like self-doubt and fear of failure.

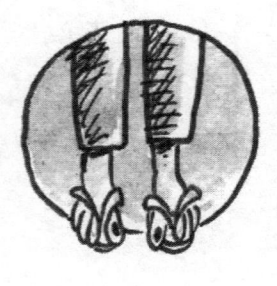

FOR MORE RESOURCES DON'T FORGET OUR WEBSITE: www.barefootguide.org

UNLEARNING

Often the biggest hindrances to new learning are things we already know, believe and want. We cling to what used to work, sometimes for good reason, but if the needs and situation have changed we may have to go through a difficult process of letting go old ways to clear the space for new ideas, beliefs and desires to take root. (See the U-Process in Chapter 5, page 112)

LEFT BRAIN / RIGHT BRAIN LEARNING

Connected to head level learning, we need to stimulate not only our left brain, where our logical, scientific, analytical thinking lies, but also our right brains, where our creative, artistic and intuitive capabilities lie. Most people lack confidence expressing their creative side so this often needs particular attention.

WISDOM

Wisdom is an ability that we all have and that comes from good experience and thoughtfulness. When we are being wise we are drawing from our experience (good and bad) to see below the surface to the truth of something and communicate that truth in word and action. Wisdom comes from the ability to deeply observe or listen, to cut through all the complexity, the information overload, to find the simpler essences and truths.

> *I would not give a fig for the simplicity on this side of complexity. But I would give my life for the simplicity on the other side.*
>
> Oliver Wendell Holmes

TYPES OF LEARNING

Learning can come in many ways, different approaches, methods and work at different levels. Here are some of the key approaches to learning to keep in mind when designing learning processes:

ACTION LEARNING – LEARNING FROM EXPERIENCE

(see Chapter 5, see pages 108–110)

In action learning we experience something, reflect on it, draw learnings, plan a new or improved approach, try this out and then again we reflect and learn again in continuous and improving cycles.

We use action learning most of the time, often unconsciously. It is the most natural way we learn. If we become more conscious of how we learn we can improve the quality of our learning.

There is **shallow action learning** – where we use trial-and-error – e.g. we try a technique and if it does not work we try another, until we find one that works...

There is **deep action learning** – where we observe what we are doing or have done, reflect on it and draw learnings, before deciding what to do differently.

"Learning can come in many ways."

CHAPTER SEVEN: STAYING ALIVE TO CHANGE

Sometimes shallow, trial-and-error learning is the better way, where conditions are simpler, the variables few and the cost of failure is low; and sometimes deep learning is better where the situation is complex and repeated failure is not an option.

HORIZONTAL LEARNING

This is related to action learning but involves learning from the experiences of others, not only your own experiences. For example peer learning, community exchanges or farmer learning groups – are particularly powerful forms of learning, very practical and rapid. This kind of learning can also reduce community isolation and build good relationships of solidarity.

Story-telling is a powerful method for horizontal learning.

VERTICAL LEARNING

From courses, schools, universities, books etc.. This is vertical learning where experts, teachers, lecturers, authors etc. teach us useful knowledge and skills that they have acquired.

Self-study can be very empowering and enables people to make use of flexible, available time. But many people need support from a coach or a mentor or even a peer study group, to enable them to succeed.

INTEGRATED LEARNING AND WORKING

All of the above types of learning have a role in the development of individuals and of organisations. Many good learning processes use more than one type and connect them strongly to actual work. For example, courses that provide a mix of horizontal and vertical learning processes, allow participants to get the best of both approaches.

Practical guidelines for designing learning

As a leader or facilitator you have a responsibility for ensuring that learning processes are fruitful, enjoyable

WORK IN DIVERSE WAYS

When designing our organisational learning processes, it is important that we are able to work at the different levels of learning and to use the different types of learning (mentioned above) that work in different situations.

Not only will the learning experiences be more fruitful but you will find that people enjoy being stimulated at different levels. Begin with simple approaches. Ask people what good learning experiences they have had and try these out, experiment with them.

Peer or horizontal learning is particularly powerful. Arranging learning exchanges can bring surprising and useful new insights and relationships between participants.

"Learning exchanges can bring surprising and useful new insights and relationships between participants."

USE LOCAL RITUALS, ACTIVITIES AND METAPHORS

Connecting with local culture helps to build trust in the group and safety in the learning processes so that people can feel free to share. If people are going to want to share their experiences and ideas they must not fear they will be criticised, laughed at or punished for being honest. A safe culture may take some time to develop, but do everything you can to protect people's right to speak honestly.

BE GROUNDED IN REAL EXPERIENCES

There is always much to be gained from people's stories, their real experiences. Help people to ask good questions of their experiences – see the 'Asking better questions' on page 25 and the 'Action learning cycle guiding questions' on page 110.

LINK LEARNING TO NEW ACTION

As people learn things, prompt them to link what they have learnt to activities, even if it is just the next step. Encourage people to experiment, to try new ideas out, to apply new learnings to their work, and to keep reflecting on their new experiences.

MAKE LEARNING FUN

Intersperse the more serious sessions with lighter activities, whether they are games, eating together, singing together, going somewhere together... learning can be tiring, so we need to vary the methods, pace, rhythm and even the settings.

"Connecting with the local culture helps build trust."

"Learning can be tiring, so we need to vary the methods, pace, rhythm and even the settings."

CHAPTER SEVEN: STAYING ALIVE TO CHANGE

Watch out for...

WALL-TO-WALL BURN-OUT

If an organisation spends 4 weeks a month hard at work how productive are they in reality? They might do more work, but do they get more work done? We have come across so many organisations that work incredibly hard at doing many things that are not really worth doing any longer, repeating the same mistakes and struggling to find funding for programmes that have become tired and lifeless. Often their staff are unhappy and many regularly get burnt out and leave. It is tragic really, because generally these organisations are filled with highly competent and committed individuals, good people who really could make a difference.

Most organisations are alike in one way - none of them take organisational learning seriously. Time put aside for peer learning is regarded as a luxury for them, something to squeeze in between "real work" if at all, *rather than seeing learning as a vital part of the whole cycle of work.*

STAR LEARNER SYNDROME

Why is it that organisations with particularly impressive leaders, who are highly experienced and empowered individuals, so often fail to live up to expectations...? One reason is that these leaders often don't feel they need to pay attention to organisational learning because, well, they already know what to do and when they don't they simply figure it all out on their own. They expect everyone else to behave in the same way, because this is how they have always done it. They are known as Star Learners, usually highly effective, admired and respected individuals.

"The work of social change has become too complex for this style of individual 'star learning' to work."

There are four problems or issues here.

...Firstly, the work of social change has become too complex for this style of individual "star learning" to work – these days organisational work requires multiple inputs and collective thinking to "figure things out".

...Secondly, most of us are not "star learners". We usually struggle to learn on our own and need to share our experiences, get feedback and have good discussions to develop our observations, insights and plans. And we are social beings who enjoy learning together.

...Thirdly, in our collaborative learning relationships and learning spaces we get a chance to play with and experiment with different viewpoints and ideas. We also get to learn about each other. If "star learner" leaders do not encourage or participate in these activities then they rob the organisation of this important foundation for effective collaborative work.

...Fourthly, if our star leaders are not with us when we learn (which may involve improving or rethinking our work) then we may develop good ideas that they don't understand, setting the stage for conflicting approaches to work. Their absence may make us insecure and prevent us from thinking and planning for ourselves.

Why do organisations resist learning?

TOO BUSY
"I am here to work... we are too busy to invest that much time.. learning is a luxury!"

We need to see learning as part of the cycle of work... just as we need to eat and sleep, to nourish and replenish ourselves, so we need to reflect and learn to feed our work with new energy and ideas.

BAD EXPERIENCES
"Last time we did a case study I was criticised and felt shamed!"

Honest learning requires a safe place, an enjoyable place of camaraderie where we can tell the truth and support and learn from each other, without fear.

BORING PROCESSES
"We had a reflection but it turned into a boring meeting!"

We need to equip ourselves with creative and effective learning processes and facilitation skills.

TOO DIFFICULT TO GET STARTED
"We don't know where to start, its too difficult"

Start with things you are already doing that help, no matter how informal or formal. Make these more conscious and try to improve on them. Perhaps in your weekly meetings, or informally in the kitchen, after work or on your way back from the field you may be having really useful conversations that help you to learn from experience. Think about how you can improve them. Who else can be included?

WHERE IS EVERYBODY?
"We tried to do it, but not everyone in the team came so we stopped" and "It seemed that learning was only for some – the "important" people didn't have time to learn with us."

This is hard and requires real leadership to convince everyone of the need to invest in collective learning.

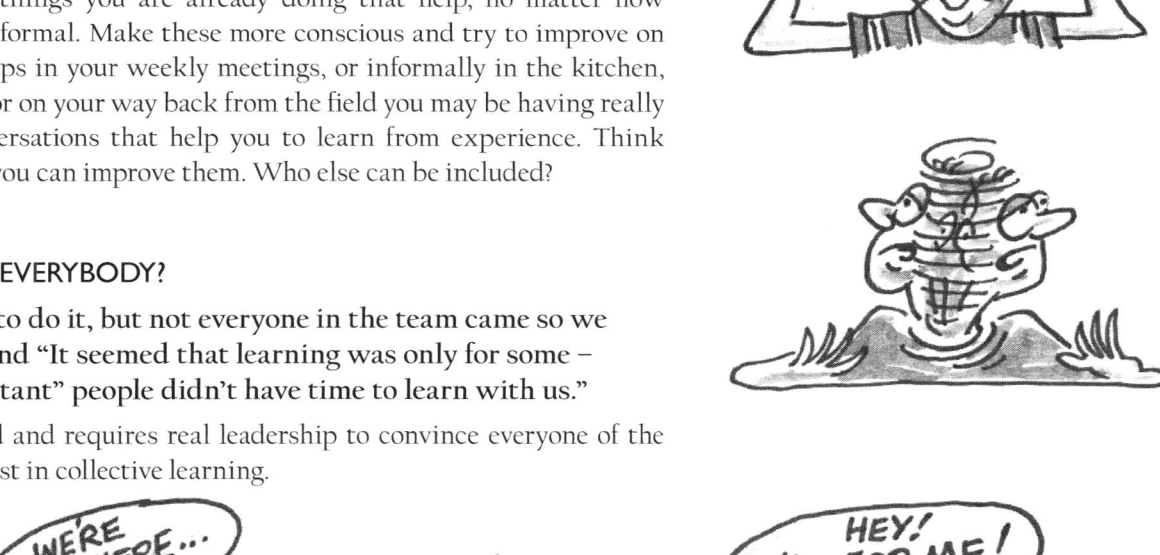

CHAPTER SEVEN: STAYING ALIVE TO CHANGE

CDRA'S SANDRA HILL TALKS ABOUT HOME WEEKS ...

"One way to be a learning organisation is to put aside regular time for members of the organisation to get together to learn."

FOR MORE RESOURCES DON'T FORGET OUR WEBSITE: www.barefootguide.org

One way to be a learning organisation is to put aside regular time for members of the organisation to get together to learn. At CDRA, we have a 'Home Week', a week-long organisational learning process which we hold almost every month of every year. All staff, both field and office based, attend. Each home-week follows a basic pattern, but not a strict routine:

MONDAY A day of re-connecting with each other, sharing breakfast and news followed by a creative workshop, run by an artist. We have done singing, painting, sculpting, drumming, dancing, etc. In the afternoon we write short 2-page reflective reports on our experience of a particular work-related theme.

TUESDAY We share our reflective reports with each other. The emphasis is not on problem-solving or advice giving – but on careful listening, observing and reflecting back what is heard and learnt. Over the years, most of our learnings have come through these reflective processes.

WEDNESDAY Case studies, a review of a paper written for a conference or publication, or an opportunity for teams to get together to workshop a course design or research initiative.

THURSDAY Business meeting focused on programme management, financial information and other internal matters, followed by a strategic allocation meeting to consider requests, queries, networking contacts and invitations. We sometimes have personal supervision on this day.

FRIDAY A study group on an important book to deepen our practice, followed by a wrap-up of outstanding issues and 'harvesting' of our reflections and conversations for future action.

CDRA has been holding home-weeks for 15 years. Putting this time aside really helps us to focus and deepen our practice.. The "recipe" we follow is constantly evolving but has the following key ingredients:

Key elements of organisational learning

1. Identify and honour your guiding principles

Some of our key principles are to pay close attention to our own experience and to learn from our own actions; to *find our own answers* as individuals and as teams; that learning is more likely to lead to change when it involves "the whole person" – head, heart and feet.

2. Find your individual and organisational questions

We ask: What strikes me as significant? What challenges me? And, what picture is emerging? We ask questions that help us move to action, such as: what implications are suggested for the future? what does this mean for me, my organisation, my practice? At CDRA we have a broad organisational question which reflects our purpose, guides our work and focuses our organisational learning: "What are the forms and processes of organisation that shift power in the world?"

3. Create opportunity to find and express voice

We believe that when you find your voice, you find your power. How do I find my voice? How do I know what I think? At CDRA we have found it useful to make time to write. Brainstorming, 'flash writing' and keeping journals help us stay awake to what's going on in the day and in ourselves. We often give time for people to think on their own. We have recently started using practice journals to log experiences and reflections as we work, for harvesting in home weeks.

4. Understand the nature of community and nurture it

Healthy relationships are vital for learning, enabling risk sharing, honesty and insight without fear of destructive criticism. The interaction, conversations and disagreements between us spark off new ways of seeing things, new ideas and new understanding. Organisational learning happens *between* us. The better the relationships, the safer the space and the more willing each of us is to share our *voice*.

5. Learn creatively and make the link between art and development

We believe that working with art forms helps us to learn with our whole brain, both its left *and* its right side. Creative processes help shift us from rational, logical, intellectual, *left-brain* thinking, towards the more imaginative, creative and intuitive thinking of the *right brain*. When we use our whole brain we are more likely to reach insights, see the bigger picture and remember that we are working into the *unknown*.

6. Support learning with leadership

Home weeks are led by a small team of three who consult staff and plan for each process, ensuring continuity and depth.

"The illiterate of the 21st century will not be those who cannot read and write, but those who cannot learn, unlearn, and relearn."
Alvin Toffler

Stories, learning and social change...

> *" The ancient ones plait their stories into the futures of their children. "*
>
> From *Ancient Ones* by Lebogang Mashile

What do folk-tales, gossip, movies, jokes, case studies and novels all have in common? They are all different kinds of stories. Can you imagine a day in your life that does not involve the telling of a story or two? Indeed, our lives are unfolding dramas, stories with past and present chapters and some future chapters waiting to be written.

We all loved stories as a children, and since the dawn of time they have played a key role in children's development. But why and how? When we tell stories they enter our children and expand them, opening up spaces in which their imaginations can explore, fly and grow, where they can lose themselves, where they can recreate themselves and try out new truths. For children, we know that stories are effective teachers, seeping under locked doors, under their resistance to instruction, becoming their own experience, their own lessons to resolve. It is a way that children have learnt through the ages, in all cultures.

Are adults any different? When we hear a good story, an interesting experience, it can wake us up to something new and if it is well told we become witnesses as the stories enter us, as with children, to become a part of our own experience to learn from.

Good learning processes always draw from some kind of experience, from stories, to feed our thinking and ideas for future action. If we want to work with learning in organisations and social change, we have to learn to work with people' stories, with their experiences. After all, social change is about people changing their lives, learning from past stories in order to change their future stories.

We learn from listening to stories but we also change and transform ourselves from telling them. When abused women from the slums of Mexico City or the townships of South Africa tell their stories to each other they transform their stories of victimisation to stories of survival and out of these create new stories of empowerment.

Anyone can tell a story – we do it all the time – when we tell our spouse what happened at work, when we explain to a child why something is dangerous, when we tell a friend about something strange that we have seen. And, like anything else, the more we practice, the better we get at it. We can write it or record it for others to read or hear.

The world is full of accomplished storytellers – artists, writers, dancers, actors, singers – they are all telling us stories. And many communities still have traditional storytellers. Seek these people out, invite them in, learn from them.

Planning, Monitoring and Evaluation (PME)

> We have been dilettantes and amateurs
> With some of our greatest notions
> For human betterment.
> We have been like spoilt children:
> We have been like tyrannical children;
> Demanding proof when listening is required.

From *Mental Fight*, by Ben Okri

This section takes a look at some of the deeper challenges of Planning, Monitoring and Evaluation (PME) approaches and activities through which organisations manage, improve, rethink and account for their practice.

OK... Time to Change the Way We Think....

> Unless mistakes or failures are being made the process is not active enough.
>
> Coenraad van Houten

We have become obsessed with RESULTS and OUTCOMES. The Development Project has become the dominant form of development organisation, often replacing local organisations. Projects demand that we put effort into predicting outcomes, results, impacts, often years ahead of time.

The assumption (and hope!) is that by being clear what we want at "the end", we will be clear about what we need to do to get there.

We assume this will provide good direction.

And we assume this will make us more accountable for these results but sadly we are usually wrong!

Sometimes, outcomes-based planning works, when the conditions are favourable, or projectable (see page 20-21)... but if not then development Projects often impose a false logic, assuming conditions that do not exist and burdening people with over-ambitious and unlikely outcomes and plans.

CHAPTER SEVEN: STAYING ALIVE TO CHANGE

MANAGEMENT BY RESULTS

To put it simply, in the complex world of social change, "Management by Results" often creates more hindrances than helps. Why?

Confusion and disappointment arise between donors and partners.

Recipients of donor funding are always having to explain why the original plan did not work, why it "failed".

We may become closed to what is possible but not predictable.

Unexpected results are often the most interesting things that happen. How often we ignore unplanned results that could have huge impact if they had been supported as they emerged.

Being driven by a strong need for results creates a destructive fear or anxiety.

What if we don't achieve these specific results? Will we get more funding? Will I get that promotion?

What is supposed to be a carrot becomes a stick – fear undermines honesty. And so, when the time comes to "measure our performance", we look for and "find" our planned results even if they are not really there. In this way, we become subtly dishones. Even more importantly, *this undermines learning from experience!* If, because of fear of failure, we cannot be fully honest, we can never learn well and therefore never improve.

So what alternatives are there?

When conditions are not predictable or projectable it is still important to have a purpose and even some objectives, but ones that are not too specific or time-bound. For example, a local development initiative in an informal settlement may have the purpose of surfacing and strengthening local women's leadership and trusting relationships as a basis for community organisation, but exactly who the women will be or how long it will take or how to achieve this or even how possible this is, may be completely uncertain. Staying open to all possible outcomes, learning from experience, may surface different possibilities that people themselves may want to pursue in preference to or in addition to the original purpose.

So, by all means have some (flexible) results or outcomes that you want to achieve... but more importantly focus on the quality of the process of change and how everyone learns on the way, enabling a continual improving and rethinking to take place.

If we can be less obsessed with results and more interested in creating the conditions for relationships and practices of honest, collaborative learning, there is a higher likelihood that we will create an organisation that discovers and then demonstrates what it is capable of, that really does produce results.

The PME Cycle and Action Learning

PLANNING
Planning is a process that clarifies the intentions and purpose of organisations and develops approaches and activities to achieve these. Planning has two components: Strategic Planning and Operational Planning.

MONITORING
This is the shorter-term continuous process of reflecting on experience to ensure that work is still on track towards meeting purpose. It involves reflecting on what is happening, drawing learnings, improving practice and enabling ongoing replanning to take place.

EVALUATION
This is the longer-term cycle of learning and re-thinking the work of the organisation, and the organisation of work, based on experience and progress over time.

We have already touched on the fundamentals of Planning, Monitoring and Evaluation (PME) in Chapter 4 (pages 91 to 93).

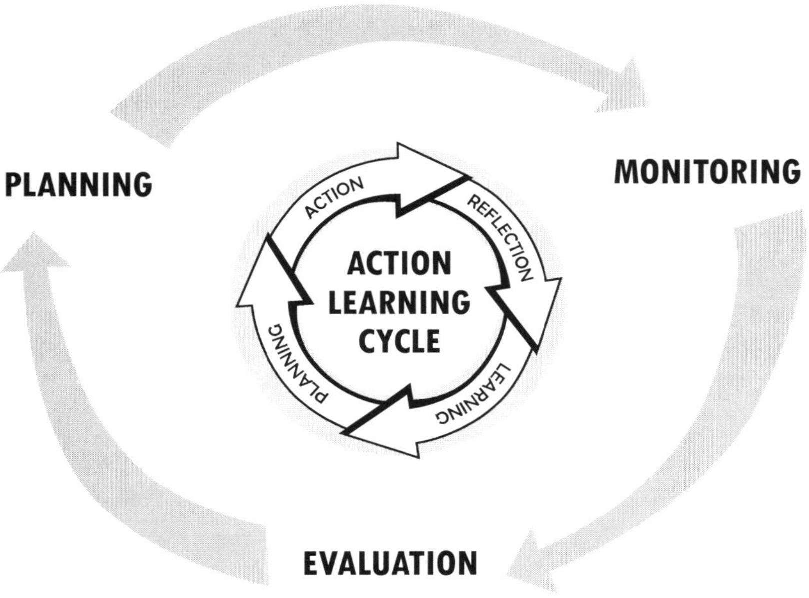

PLANNING → **MONITORING** → **EVALUATION**

ACTION LEARNING CYCLE
ACTION → REFLECTION → LEARNING → PLANNING

A PME cycle is essentially a form of an Action Learning cycles (see pages 109–110) applied to organisational support for practice.

"RUN LIKE HELL!"
"IT'S PME TIME AGAIN!"
"HUFF PUFF"
"WAIT! STOP!" — PME

CHAPTER SEVEN: STAYING ALIVE TO CHANGE

WHY DO WE NEED PME?

Planning, monitoring, evaluating and reporting helps us to manage, improve, rethink and account for our practice, over time. Let's take a closer look at each of these:

MANAGING PRACTICE

Through cycles of planning, monitoring and replanning we are able to keep track of what we do and make necessary adjustments – rather like a ship's steersman keeping a hand on the ship's wheel, one eye on the compass and one eye on the horizon, constantly adjusting and checking to keep the ship on course.

IMPROVING PRACTICE

Through good monitoring and evaluating processes (we could just as well say short-term and long-term learning) we can reflect on our experience, learn from our mistakes, capitalise on our successes, deepen our understanding of our work and continuously develop, strengthen and enhance our practice.

RETHINKING PRACTICE

Through good evaluation, whether short- or long-term we are able to rethink our practice – as the context and needs change, and as we change. It does seem that the context is getting more and more changeable these days requiring us to rethink almost continuously.

ACCOUNTING (AND REPORTING) FOR PRACTICE

We do not work in isolation. If we are leading or assisting people then we should be accountable to them for the quality of our leadership or help, to ensure that we are doing no harm. The best way to do this is to get and give honest feedback.

If we are getting funds from others we need to account for these. Donors are understandably anxious for proof of results, but they are more likely to get results if they ask for a different kind of proof:

Firstly, donors can ask for an honest account of the use of resources (ie. financial audits)

Secondly, an honest account of our experiences and learnings and how we are translating these learning into improving or rethinking our practice – in other words proof that good effort is being put into managing, improving and rethinking practice.

Mapping PME in the Development Sector

FINDING OUR CHALLENGES

Discussions about PME can be confusing and frustrating. One reason is because we don't realise that there are many layers to PME, so we often talk at cross-purposes. In the diagram below we depict the 3 main actors, but between them there are 5 layers of PME – each actor has their own PME systems, to manage, improve, rethink and account their own practice... and then each has a PME relationship with actors above or below them... have a good look at the diagram here. See what you make of the challenges of each actor (these are just a few!).

PME AND REPORTING UP AND DOWN THE DEVELOPMENT SECTOR

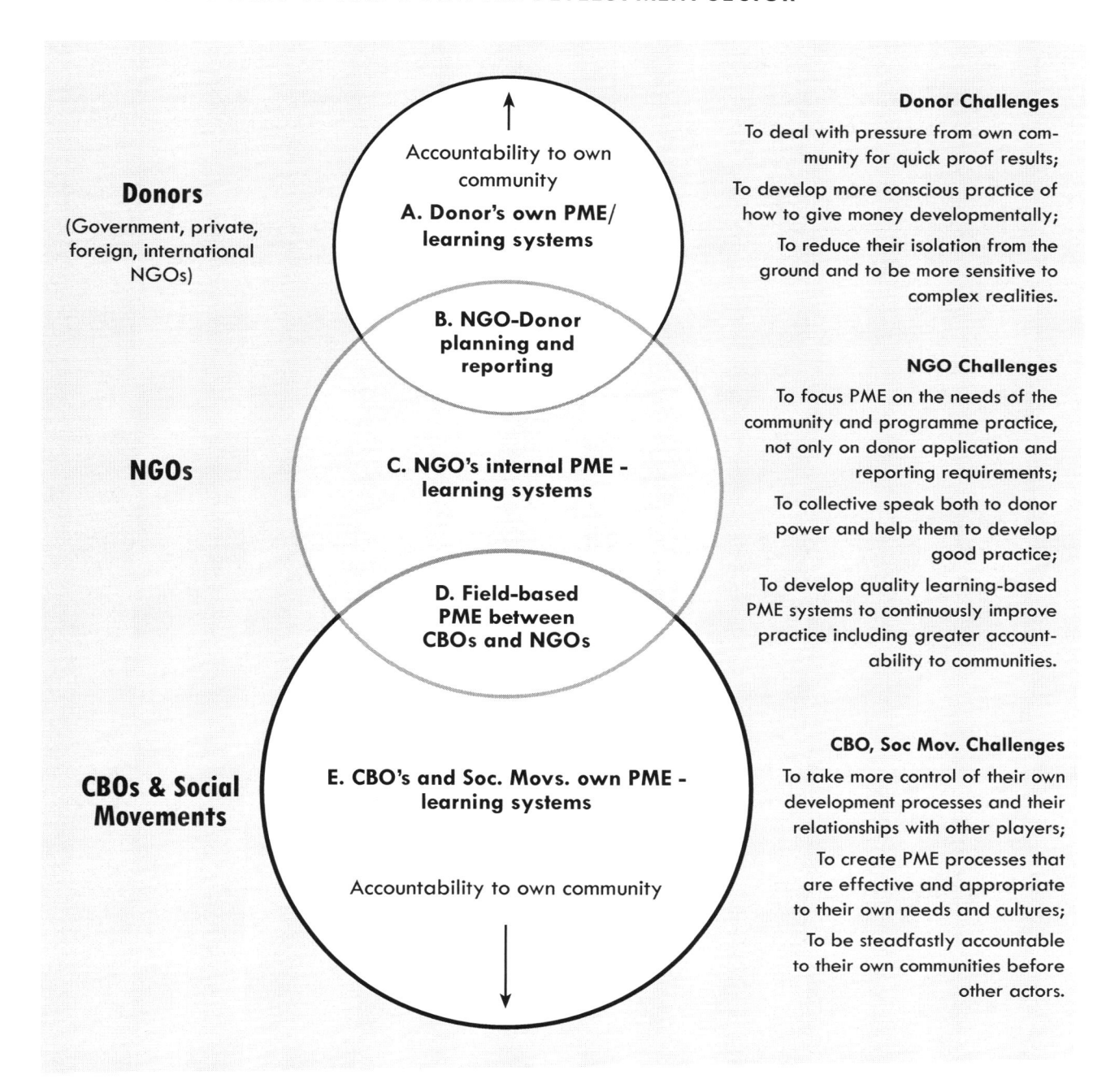

Donors
(Government, private, foreign, international NGOs)

NGOs

CBOs & Social Movements

Accountability to own community

A. Donor's own PME/learning systems

B. NGO-Donor planning and reporting

C. NGO's internal PME – learning systems

D. Field-based PME between CBOs and NGOs

E. CBO's and Soc. Movs. own PME – learning systems

Accountability to own community

Donor Challenges
To deal with pressure from own community for quick proof results;
To develop more conscious practice of how to give money developmentally;
To reduce their isolation from the ground and to be more sensitive to complex realities.

NGO Challenges
To focus PME on the needs of the community and programme practice, not only on donor application and reporting requirements;
To collective speak both to donor power and help them to develop good practice;
To develop quality learning-based PME systems to continuously improve practice including greater accountability to communities.

CBO, Soc Mov. Challenges
To take more control of their own development processes and their relationships with other players;
To create PME processes that are effective and appropriate to their own needs and cultures;
To be steadfastly accountable to their own communities before other actors.

CHAPTER SEVEN: STAYING ALIVE TO CHANGE

Exploring PME in more depth

PLANNING

Planning is a process that clarifies the intentions and purpose of organisations.

It makes conscious and converts into action the very identity of an organisation. It must therefore be done in a way that is appropriate and meaningful to the organisation itself.

- As an imagined projection into the future, plans must be expected to change as implementation progresses and learning takes place. All plans should be regarded as being in draft form, ready for re-planning.

- Those requiring the plans of others (like donors) must develop the skill to interpret the plans of their partners into the "language" and framework that they need to use and not force their partners to do it in ways that are not appropriate to them.

Local planning approaches should be encouraged.

MONITORING

Good monitoring shows a genuine interest in what is being done and a constant and curious questioning of activities and their emerging effects.

Monitoring (with learning) involves a commitment to standing back from the doing from time to time to see how it is going in relation to what was imagined and planned.

Monitoring should be seen as a reflective practice that assists learning to take place, enabling improvement in practice, including possible rethinking and replanning. It can also be an important affirming practice of what is going well.

If monitoring is separated from learning it risks becoming a policing function.

EVALUATING

Evaluating is a process of reviewing and assessing the value of something.

It differs from monitoring in that it goes beyond and behind the implementation of activities to assess impact against deeper purpose and intention. Evaluation is inherently threatening as it brings into question issues of identity and fundamental reason for being. If done well it is a source of the most profound insights and learning.

- Evaluating should always be owned and controlled by the organisation that will draw learning from it. You can help us to evaluate ourselves, but you cannot realistically evaluate me and expect me to learn from it.

- Outsiders can play a valuable role as facilitators and questioners.

- Evaluation should always be accompanied by a facilitated process that allows the organisation or community to come to its own final conclusions and plan its own change process based on its learning.

- The quality of the evaluation report should be de-emphasised as an indication of the quality of an evaluation. The contribution towards increased learning understanding and improved practice should be the gauge. Good evaluation should lead to a feeling of greater self-control and responsibility.

- Independent evaluations that attempt to impose recommendations by outside experts can severely undermine the growing sovereignty of an organisation.

- Practitioners may be able to demonstrate and illustrate impact downstream through following up particular case studies, but scientifically measuring results or impacts downstream requires research, with skills, resources and time that average practitioners do not normally have. Donors need to be funding research for this impact on ultimate and wider "beneficiaries", relieving the pressure on PM&E systems sothat organisations can focus on learning. (see the next section on Outcome Mapping for an elaboration of this point)

Evaluations can only hope to assess the impact of interventions on those most directly affected.

Outcome mapping

A DEVELOPMENTAL APPROACH TO PME
by Christine Mylks, Terry Smutylo and Doug Reeler

BEHIND OUTCOME MAPPING

Many of us are familiar with the pressure to monitor and evaluate our work in order to assess whether our efforts have made people's lives better. Often this kind of change or 'impact' is far from where we work and depends on the actions of others too. The pathways linking our work to the better world we seek have many twists and turns – as well as many other travellers. We work in complex situations where sustained changes in well-being usually result from multiple factors, both positive and negative. Disentangling our contribution from other influences is a major challenge in all monitoring and evaluation.

For example, an evaluation may identify an improvement in the health of children two years after the initiation of a child health education programme with traditional healers. But can we say that the programme was the only cause of the improvement without researching everything else that happened in the lives of the children over the two years? Our work with traditional healers may have been a factor in the health improvement but it is possible that it was only a small and insignificant contribution amongst several other more important factors. Improved crop yields, vaccinations, increased use of bed nets, none of which may be connected to our work, can make huge contributions to the health of children. Or our programme may have been significant only because of the contributions of other interventions – perhaps a change in the way the Ministry of Health allocates its resources.

EVALUATING IMPACT

Measuring the causes of 'impact' within the complex processes of development can require research resources and skills far beyond the capacity of a programme's monitoring and evaluation (M&E) activities. In fact, using our limited monitoring and evaluation systems for impact evaluation can be dangerously misleading if we do not recognize and understand the importance of other significant contributions.

While logframes and other logic models may be useful for simplifying and summarizing the rationale and components of a program for communicating with some audiences, they do not offer an adequate basis for monitoring and evaluation. They often offer false hope that a single program can actually achieve 'impact' all by itself. The simplicity of logic models can help us illustrate how a particular intervention is supposed to work. However, when it comes to measuring our results, this simplicity often misleads us by leaving out the emergent, complex, web-like or even circular ways that social change and organisational transformation really happen.

Unfortunately, many programmes are required, by their sponsoring organizations, to use monitoring and evaluation to "prove" that their efforts have brought about lasting changes for poor people. The time and effort that goes into this tends to distract us from a deeper understanding of the messiness of development, from exploring and learning how to "improve" the way we work within our organisations and communities.

OUTCOME MAPPING AS A DEVELOPMENTAL ALTERNATIVE

Originally developed by the International Development Research Centre in Ottawa, Canada, Outcome Mapping is based on twenty years of learning from field work in many corners of the world.

Here are a few words from IDRC about OM:

> *The focus of Outcome Mapping is on people and organizations. The originality of the methodology is its shift away from assessing the products of a program (e.g., policy relevance, poverty alleviation, reduced conflict) to focus on changes in behaviours, relationships, actions, and/or activities of the people and organizations with whom a development program works directly.*

For more on Outcome Mapping, you can join the online learning community at www.outcomemapping.ca

TRACKING INCREMENTAL CHANGE

OM directs us to pay attention to behaviours and relationships relevant to the changes in conditions we seek to bring about. It gives us a way to make tangible and track the incremental changes in the way people and organizations act relative to the overall direction we want to go in. The OM focus on what happens within our immediate 'sphere of influence' enables us to measure the relationship between our interventions and the corresponding changes in how people treat each other and the ecosystem. It also helps us avoid the trap that many M&E systems lure us into of claiming we "caused" changes far beyond our reach, changes which involved many other actors, changes way 'downstream' from where we are actually working.

"BOUNDARY PARTNERS" AND LEARNING

Our "Boundary Partners" are those groups, organizations or individuals we work with, who are impacted by our work with them, directly. We can see the impact of our work to the extent that they have benefited (or not) from our support or influence.

They are the best measurers of our impact because they should themselves be able to tell what effects you have had, giving you direct feedback, thus allowing us to gauge the effectiveness of our practice and gain some insight into the likely or possible effects downstream. But our boundary partners also have their own boundary partners who they try to influence. Using this way of thinking, may help them gauge the likely contributions they make to the actions or well-being of the groups they work with. It will help them develop a deeper understanding of the context in which they function and use that understanding to improve their effectiveness. So monitoring becomes not a means to generate "proof of impact", but a way of getting useful guidance for ongoing work.

"BOUNDARY PARTNERS"

MICHAEL TRIEST SHARES THIS STORY ABOUT OUTCOME MAPPING...

Outcome Mapping (OM), it's OK now, although we weren't always enthusiastic about it, but it grew on us. Our first encounter with OM was in VVOB's project about environmental education at 3 secondary teacher education colleges in Zimbabwe – there it helped us to think about and distinguish between the project structures and the role of the locally operational donor structures. This allows for local structures to continue existing after the donor stops funding - great for sustainability, and we see that now happening.

OM guided us into agreeing on what could come out of working together in terms of "We expect to see …", "We would like to see …", and "We would love to see …" This was attractive and practical. There's the hitch now. Nothing in OM forces you to really go to the bottom of things, so it also depends on how much heart, how much bottom-up approach, how much "feeling" you organise the consultations and the cooperation. It depends on how much you really are interested in the people you work together with – as in all systems. Otherwise you just get lots of documents that look interesting but miss the point – as in all systems. The nice thing of OM is that, although you can still blow it, the approach gives you the opportunity to communicate deeply, to talk, to interact.

We are trying this now in the new 2008-2013 Quality Education and Vulnerability programme at VVOB Zimbabwe. We also put the documents temporarily aside to integrate a participatory search of what was really important to us and our partners – then to discover that the links with the OM framework were made easily. The framework, with its emphasis on "think about monitoring as from the beginning", helped a lot in organisational learning, in surfacing what we learned as the programme grows organically. That's why we like OM more than 'logical frameworks' in a complex environment.

Horizontal Learning – and new forms of organisation...

CHRISSY SHARES THIS INSPIRING STORY...

A Sideways Approach to Development

Mrs. Letela, the principal in a small rural primary school in Lesotho, stood at her office window, watching the children playing on the field outside. She was wondering what to do about the increasing number who were coming to school hungry and how tired and irritable the teachers said the children were. How could they be expected to learn? We've got hungry children, whose parents are farmers, and empty fields lying here. Surely we can do something? She started visiting some parents, asking questions, chatting to them about the idea of growing food at the school, listening to their ideas and encouraging them to speak amongst themselves. When she felt the time was ripe she invited parents to a meeting where they agreed to take responsibility for establishing a garden at the school to feed their children. But they would have to do it differently to the way they farmed, because the vegetables needed to be grown and harvested throughout the year, unlike their own annual maize crops.

Mrs. Letela asked around town at the offices of a few development organisations and was told about a regional association of NGOs, called Pelum, who promoted small-scale organic farming. She wrote to them and they soon replied, agreeing that two trainers would be sent for a few weeks to teach a group of parents an approach that would combine their own farming methods with permaculture, enabling different foods to be grown throughout the year, and without the need for costly fertilisers and pesticides. Fortunately the association had access to flexible funding that enabled them to move quickly on this request.

The trainers began by spending good time surfacing what the parents already knew about vegetable gardening, before introducing them to the essential permaculture principles and methods. Throughout the process they involved the parents in every aspect of designing and developing an integrated gardening system for the whole school garden.

It was less than two months later that all the children started getting a nutritious meal every day at school, grown by the parents and harvested and cooked by the domestic science students. And it was not long, Mrs. Letela heard, before the parents started adopting some of these farming methods in their own gardens and farms, as did she herself. Soon the word got around and a delegation of parents and teachers from the neighbouring school marched over the hill and asked if they could be taught to do the same. So parents began to teach parents, farmers learning from farmers. And it continued to spread through the district. Within three years 58 schools and communities had started similar initiatives, each taught by a neighbouring school. The idea has since spread even further, with official sanction and support, to another four districts involving a further 200 schools. A part-time advice centre was set up at Mrs. Letela's school, with one person employed on a small grant from an overseas donor, to give advice and information and to put people in touch with each other. Mrs. Letela's school has been piloting organic vegetable gardening as a part of the school curriculum.

> **QUESTIONS TO WORK WITH**
> Using the Action Learning Cycle guiding questions (on page 110), unpack this story and draw learnings and implications that may be useful for your own practice.

DUSTING OFF HORIZONTAL LEARNING

What is horizontal learning and how does it relate to other forms of learning? We have already explored action learning. As its close companion, much of what we have said for action learning is true for horizontal learning. Learning from our neighbours and peers is surely an ancient practice, as natural as action learning. Horizontal and action learning are usually intertwined, the same process – my brother showing me how he fixed his gutter, a farmer demonstrating to her neighbours how she controls cutworms or a fellow worker telling the story of how they organised, at another factory, to get medical benefits. These are all examples of both.

When Education arrived in the form of expert teachers, doctors, nurses, lawyers, agricultural extension workers etc. – for most people as part of colonial domination – the result was that people's belief in the value of their own and their neighbour's experiences, knowledge and ideas became increasingly undermined. Cultures and practices of horizontal, community learning and knowledge have become half-buried and vertical dependencies have emerged over the past few generations, continually reinforced by modern society. Knowledge and learning have become external commodities increasingly removed from the organic life of communities, robbing people not only of access to their own local knowledge and potential, but weakening the accompanying age-old interdependent relationships of community. Restoring or renewing cultures and practices of horizontal learning, hand-in-hand with action learning, surely becomes central to a developmental practice, central to purpose.

This is not to say that teachers and experts have unimportant roles. They often have both experience and knowledge that have a critical place in learning and it would be foolish to deny ourselves access to these. They can bring more conceptual clarity than is often available in the peer group, of immense value. The thing is to know when to bring it and how. New knowledge should be introduced only after own knowledge and experience is brought out, so that the new or expert knowledge can complement and expand what people already knew, rather than to ignore, deny or replace it, as so often happens.

Community elders have a role because their relationship with the learners, and their context, is usually more intimate and complex. As members of the same community they share many aspects of a peer relationship, as insiders, but also bring with them story and history, local knowledge and wisdom, culture and tradition. When these are shared they come not from the outside or above but deeply from within the community, from out of the past, revealing what already belongs to the community, its heritage and deep identity. Although there are dependencies and other power issues in relationships with elders they do represent something quite different from those between learners and professional teachers or experts.

Horizontal learning, like action learning, is another natural and innate process in which we can embed transformation.

"Horizontal learning, like action learning, is a natural and innate process in which we can embed transformation."

DIFFERENT KINDS OF HORIZONTAL LEARNING

There is a whole variety of horizontal learning approaches to social change being practised today, and more are being experimented with...

COMMUNITY KNOWLEDGE EXCHANGES

This is the most common practice we know of, usually taking the form of a community visiting another community to learn something specific – e.g. daily savings systems, how to farm snails, seed saving techniques, child-care approaches etc. The visiting community can also bring their experience and knowledge to share so that it's a more equal exchange.

PEER LEARNING GROUPS

Like the Farmer Learning Groups described below (page 160), these are often closer, ongoing groups, sharing real experiences, innovations and learnings.

Knowledge Exchanges and Peer Learning Groups can lead to joint programmes and even to networks, movements, federations, unions etc through which smaller groups unite to tackle bigger systemic problems.

SAVINGS AND CREDIT SCHEMES

These are savings collectives that form themselves into economic solidarity cooperatives. There are widespread practices of savings groups inspiring and teaching new groups to form and then wider movements of groups banding together to mobilise larger loans and access resources and to even to form social movements to engage government in policy change and implementation

SURVEYS AND DATA-GATHERING

Locally run horizontal, participative surveys gathering, distilling and sharing information about the community - its make-up, problems, possibilities and needs - to inform both local initiatives and as information with which to engage government.

FARMER-LED RESEARCH

Farmer-led research engages participative approaches to investigating, experimenting and innovating in local practices, taking horizontal learning to a more disciplined level of practice.

LEARNING FAIRS AND FESTIVALS

Where people openly gather in festive occasion to promote and share their knowledge and innovations with each other.

"Restoring or renewing cultures and practices of horizontal learning, hand-in-hand with action learning, surely becomes central to a developmental practice, central to purpose."

CHAPTER SEVEN: STAYING ALIVE TO CHANGE

CHRISSY SHARES ANOTHER INSPIRING STORY...

Story of the Tanzanian farmers

The NGO in Tanzania had for decades attempted to teach farmers modern methods learned in the agricultural colleges of the North. But those who had accepted the new methods had not done particularly well, in fact many were poorer, whereas others who had accepted and then ignored the advice, had not done badly. Eventually a new generation of Tanzanian trainers realised that between them the farmers knew more about farming under local conditions than they did and decided to change their approach.

They started to prompt farmers to form Farmer Learning Groups, not quite sure what it would lead to. Farmers were encouraged to meet regularly and to share their working methods and innovations, and to invite into their company some of the older farmers who had stubbornly held on to their time-worn methods and less productive but drought-resistant seeds. The trainers (now facilitators) did not insist on any formality or committees or minute-taking, just meeting each other to share what they knew. It took a little while for the first groups to find their own process, to work out how they wanted to learn together, but this they did and it began to lead to the kind of improved practices the NGO had long been trying to promote. The facilitators, with the farmers' permission, started to document and publish these methods and innovations, in comic form, in Swahili, making them available, with the story of their origins, to a wider group of people.

Soon they were being approached by more farmers for help to set up similar learning groups and were able to draw on established Farmer Learning Groups to help, but they also heard of groups elsewhere that had started up spontaneously. Most surprising was that some Farmer Learning Groups, completely unprompted, were embarking on joint farming development projects while others were electing representatives to approach the local council to ask for services that were due to them, especially better roads and marketing facilities. And it was not long before some of the groups banded together and formed themselves into branches of Mviwata, the national independent small farmers union.

> *"The facilitators, with the farmers' permission, started to document and publish these methods and innovations, in comic form, in Swahili."*

WWW.BAREFOOTGUIDE.ORG

THE ROLE OF EXTERNAL FACILITATORS

Many horizontal learning processes like community exchanges and farmer learning groups require a very different role from supportive practitioners.

PREPARATION

Before the process there is often much preparation, e.g. helping participants to be clear about the purpose of the exchange, supporting the planning and logistics associated with travel and food, if needed, helping to mobilise resources etc.

SUPPORT

After the process a practitioner can give support in the application of learnings, to implementing plans

MEETINGS AND SHARING

During the process it is important that the culture of meeting and sharing of participants holds sway, rather than "Western workshop" cultures. Indeed many of the most successful exchanges are not facilitated by an outsider.

What we have learnt about Horizontal Learning

Horizontal Learning processes are often quite messy. At community level good knowledge exchanges seldom work if they are facilitated workshops. Exchanges often work best within local rituals and culture where community learners find their own ways of sharing experiences and knowledge.

LESS HIERARCHICAL Horizontal Learning processes can encourage the emergence of leadership that is less hierarchical and more facilitative and empowering.

SHARING We have also seen heightened attitudes and behaviours of ownership amongst participants and an increased willingness for sharing of risk and responsibility.

INDIGENOUS KNOWLEDGE Horizontal learning processes recognise organic or indigenous knowledge and practices, valuing the knowledge of doers and not only of thinkers. Recognises, values and mobilises the diversity of practices and forms of knowing. The valuing of informal, of more indigenous and cultural processes of learning.

SYNERGY A shift from satisfaction of singular needs to the synergistic satisfaction of several needs.

CHAPTER SEVEN: STAYING ALIVE TO CHANGE

> *"Horizontal learning processes recognise organic or indigenous knowledge and practices, valuing the knowledge of doers and not only of thinkers."*

FOR MORE RESOURCES DON'T FORGET OUR WEBSITE: www.barefootguide.org

INTERACTION Enables peer support and empathy. Provides safer, more human and open spaces for more natural human interaction.

AUTHENTIC Authentic exchanges with sufficient diversity often surface crises and conflict through which transformative shifts can be experienced.

CULTURAL EXCHANGE Learning exchanges are significantly enhanced by cultural exchange.

SHARING REAL STORIES

Sharing real stories and demonstrating things in a situation and atmosphere of friendliness, kindness and trust sets the scene for new levels of learning and development. Stories enable the listeners to re-experience the stories and activities and enter the lives of the story-tellers, gaining new experiences to learn from and catalysing experiential learning for all involved. Out of this heightened and common understandings can emerge. This is not a modern idea but has likely been the natural lifeblood of healthy community development since time immemorial.

ONE LAST STORY TO END OFF WITH...

We heard a case story from a small-farmer/community-worker in the Limpopo province of how a group of 60-odd villages revived a traditional practice of meeting once a year for a seed-sharing festival. This had fallen into disuse since the agricultural industry, ushered in by government extension officers, began showing small farmers the modern way, creating deep and worrying dependencies on corporate-controlled seeds, fertilisers and pesticides. An awareness workshop by a local NGO on the looming dangers of genetically-modified seed finally tipped the scales and provoked the renewal of the old practice.

Now, at a different village each year, the farmers once again send representatives of each village to gather and congregate for several days, each bringing sacks of their beans and grains to cook and taste and then to freely share as seed, with advice on how best to plant and grow. And all of this generates the revival of other cultural practices, of songs and dances and stories that express a renewed identity of community and interdependency.

SEEDS OF A GLOBAL COMMUNITY

CHAPTER SEVEN: STAYING ALIVE TO CHANGE

WHEN SOMEONE DEEPLY LISTENS TO YOU

When someone deeply listens to you
it is like holding out a dented cup
you've had since childhood
and watching it fill up with
cold, fresh water.
When it balances on top of the brim,
you are understood.
When it overflows and touches your skin,
you are loved.

When someone deeply listens to you
the room where you stay
starts a new life
and the place where you wrote
your first poem
begins to glow in your mind's eye.
It is as if gold has been discovered!

When someone deeply listens to you
your barefeet are on the earth
and a beloved land that seemed distant
is now at home within you.

By John Fox
from *Finding What You Didn't Lose*
www.poeticmedicine.org

Acknowledgements

Chapter 1 – Page 21
Social Threefolding
Nicanor Perlas, *Shaping Globalisation: Civil Society, Cultural Power and Threefolding*. 2000, CADI: Philipinnes/ Globenet3: New York / Novalis: Cape Town

Chapter 2 – page 29
The Threefold Human Being
Rudolf Steiner, *The Riddles of Philosophy*, Anthroposophic Press, 1973

This archetype was used by most early religious orders as body soul and spirit but was banned by an ecclesiastical council in 869 AD. The church hierarchy felt only they should work with the spirit. Rudolf Steiner revived the use of the total concept in 1917.

Chapter 2 – page 33
Phases of Individual Development
Bernard Lievegoed, *Phases*, Rudolf Steiner Press, 1998

Chapter 2 – page 38
The Four Temperaments
Rudolf Steiner, *The Four Temperaments - 1 lecture 1909*, Anthroposophic Press, 1971

Chapter 2 – page 42
Leadership Polarities
Leo de la Houssaye of the NPI Institute of Organisation Development — we have been unable to track a reference. David Scott kindly pointed out this as a concept originally developed by Leo.

Chapter 3 – Page 8
Types of Power
Adapted from Jonathan C. Erwin, *Classroom of Choice: Giving Students What They Need and Getting What You Want*, ASCD, 2004

Chapter 3 – page 9
Bases of Power
Adapted from French, J. R. P., & Raven, B. H. (1959). *The Bases of Social Power*. In D. Cartwright (Ed.), *Studies in social power* (pp. 150-167).

Chapter 4 – Page 74
The Phases of Organisation Development
Bernard Lievegoed, B., *The Developing Organisation*, Tavistock, London, 1974.

Fritz Glasl, *The Enterprise of the Future: Moral Intuition in Leadership and Organisation Development*. Hawthorn Press, UK, 1997

Chapter 5 – Pages 108-110
Action Learning
Although Action Learning is recognised as a natural archetype of learning in the Barefoot Guide it was first theorised by Reg Revans in the 1940s. See Revans, R. 1980. Action learning: New techniques for management. London: Blond & Briggs, Ltd.

Chapter 5 – Pages 112-117
The U-process
The U-process was developed in 1970 by Glasl and Lemson -(see Glasl, F. Confronting Conflict: A First-Aid Kit for Handling Conßict, Stroud: Hawthorn Press, 1999). A different but related version of the U-process has been developed by Peter Senge, Otto Scharmer, Joseph Jaworski, and Betty Sue Flowers. Presence: Human Purpose and the Field of the Future. Cambridge, MA, SoL, 2004. We still use the older and simpler version described here, but like the action learning cycle, the U-process is a change archetype that is as old as human development itself.

Chapter 5 – Page 119
"What Can Be Done ?" by Meas Nee. An extract from his book Towards Restoring Life: Cambodian Villages. 1995, Krom Akphiwat Phum, Battambang/OSB Australia - A poetic story of remarkably respectful facilitation of development in deeply traumatised communities in Cambodia. Available on the CDRA website.

Chapter 6 – Pages 131-133
William Bridges: *Managing Transitions, making the most of change*, Addison-Wesley, Massachusetts 1991